The
JEWISH HOSPITAL &
CINCINNATI JEWS
in MEDICINE

The

JEWISH HOSPITAL & CINCINNATI JEWS *in* MEDICINE

Frederic Krome

THE
History
PRESS

Published by The History Press
Charleston, SC
www.historypress.net

Copyright © 2015 by Frederic Krome
All rights reserved

Images courtesy Henry R. Winkler Center for the History of the Health Professions unless otherwise noted.

First published 2015

Manufactured in the United States

ISBN 978.1.46711.849.1

Library of Congress Control Number: 2015945700

This book is dedicated to John Fine, Saul Benison and Henry R. Winkler. All three were my teachers, my mentors and my role models. More than that, all three were my friends. May their memory be for a blessing.

CONTENTS

PREFACE

For more than a century, the Jewish Hospital of Cincinnati was located on Burnet Avenue, on the border between the neighborhoods of Mount Auburn and Avondale. The complex was part of what locals often call "Pill Hill," for in addition to the Jewish Hospital, the area also includes the University of Cincinnati Medical School, UC Medical (formerly Cincinnati General Hospital), Cincinnati Children's Hospital, Shriner's Hospital and a branch of the Veteran Administration Hospital. Of all these institutions, however, the Jewish Hospital was the first to locate itself in this region, arguably anchoring its development.

In 1994, the Jewish Hospital of Cincinnati was sold to the Cincinnati Health Alliance, bringing to a close its nearly 150-year history as an institution sponsored and run by the Cincinnati Jewish community. Three years later, the Hospital closed its Burnet Avenue facility and moved its entire operation to a new location in Kenwood, an upscale part of the city several miles from the urban center, thereby severing another link with its past. With the breakdown of the Health Alliance, the Hospital was subsequently sold in 2010 to Mercy Health, a Catholic organization; after this latest transfer of ownership, it seemed to some that the only thing Jewish about the Jewish Hospital was its name.

Despite the institution now being under the aegis of a Catholic organization, the Mercy Health Alliance has committed itself to maintaining the Jewish identity of the Hospital. A visitor to the Kenwood facility will see the walls of the hallway near the entranceway covered with the memorial plaques that testify to

This entrance to the Jewish Hospital building was part of the 1922 expansion and was demolished in the late 1960s renovation.

a long tradition of individual giving by members of the Cincinnati Jewish community. In the twenty-first century, patients at the Jewish Hospital have access to rabbinic chaplains and kosher food—something that patients in the twentieth century could not always get. Indeed, in the 1930s, when a local rabbi asked that space in the Hospital be set aside for a chapel, the president of the Jewish Hospital Association was against it, for he asked, "Who would use it?" In the same year, when an Orthodox rabbi demanded that kosher food be served at the Hospital, he was met with a hostile response from the board, which was more concerned with the ongoing financial crisis of the Great Depression than with adhering to religious practice.

It might seem surprising that an institution founded and sustained by a Jewish community was for many years not concerned with Jewish spiritual and ritual observance in its flagship medical establishment. This begs an interesting question: if the leadership was not interested in promoting these

Sign for the Jewish Hospital at the corner of Kenwood Road and Galbraith; the Mercy Health logo is clearly visible at the lower left. *Photo by author.*

Donor plaques such as these lined the entryway of the Jewish Hospital throughout much of the twentieth century. Many were transferred to the Kenwood facility in the 1990s. *Photo by author.*

attributes of Jewish life, why then establish and maintain a Jewish hospital? Indeed, without such things as kosher food and religious observance, was the Jewish Hospital really a Jewish institution?

In order to address the question "How Jewish was the Jewish Hospital?" we must first set some of the historical parameters. One useful source is Daniel Bridge's 1985 rabbinic thesis on the history of Jewish hospitals in the United States, written while he was a student at Cincinnati's Hebrew Union College–Jewish Institute of Religion. Bridge listed five reasons why American Jewish communities founded their own hospitals:

1. They detected missionizing on the part of Christians in other hospitals.
2. They needed training positions for Jewish physicians.
3. They desired an institution that would serve kosher food and follow ritual practices.
4. They had concerns regarding the types of patients found in other hospitals.
5. They wished to imitate (and help) Christians by building similar institutions.

As we shall see in the first chapter, the desire to protect sick and dying Jews from missionaries was a major factor in the founding of the Jewish Hospital of Cincinnati. Since the Hospital was established in the mid-nineteenth century, before systematic discrimination against Jewish physicians became common, Bridge's second reason does not apply. Indeed, Bridge argued that no Jewish hospital founded in the nineteenth century was created in response to this type of discrimination. While the lack of kosher food, rabbinic services and even a chapel seem to belie the Jewish character of the institution, the issue is further clouded by the fact that even during the first decades of its existence, the Hospital accepted patients regardless of ethnicity or religious affiliation. Given that only one of these five characteristics seems to apply, what then made the institution a Jewish one?

Bridge's thesis provides another possible way of understanding how an institution can have a Jewish character, even without the myriad reasons for its being founded. In order to assess the Jewish character of an institution, Bridge suggested that some combination of nine attributes has to exist:

1. The hospital was founded by members of the Jewish community.
2. The hospital was built primarily for the members of the Jewish community.

3. The hospital was funded primarily by members of the Jewish community.
4. The hospital had a Jewish name.
5. The hospital was governed by members of the Jewish community.
6. The hospital was staffed by an unusually high percentage of Jews.
7. The hospital was viewed as "Jewish" by the Jewish community.
8. The hospital adhered to Jewish religious ritual practices to a greater degree than Christian religious practices.
9. The hospital was a place where Jewish patients could feel comfortable.

As we will see, seven of these attributes were a consistent part of the institution's life throughout the first century of its operation. Interestingly, when examining the history of the Jewish Hospital, the second and third points were not applicable. In addition to admitting non-Jewish patients, the Hospital also received a great deal of support from the non-Jewish population. It is fair to say, however, that the association relied primarily on the Jewish community for funding. Simply put, the student of history finds that in some ways the Jewish Hospital of Cincinnati does not fit into a very neat categorization of other Jewish hospitals in the United States, while in other ways it is a quintessentially Jewish organization. It is the study of these points of confluence and divergence that makes the history of the institution and the story of Jews and medicine in Cincinnati so fascinating.

The history of the Jewish Hospital of Cincinnati and Jews and medicine in Cincinnati is more than the story of a faith-based charitable medical institution and its doctors. A study of the origins and evolution of the institution, and the local medical health professionals associated with it, not only demonstrates important details about the local Jewish community but also reveals important details about the expansion of the city of Cincinnati.

While the Hospital was founded in downtown Cincinnati, its migration north into the area now known as Pill Hill was part of the trajectory of the Cincinnati Jewish community, and even its move into the suburbs reflects the changing geographic dispersal of the Jewish population—an ironic development given that the Hospital is technically no longer a communal organization.

A study of the institutional practices of the Hospital provides insights into developments in American medical history, local philanthropy and the evolution of modern concepts of management and healthcare. The history of Cincinnati's Jewish Hospital and the story of Jews and medicine

The new entranceway to the Jewish Hospital building in 1968, when the extensive rebuilding and renovation was almost complete.

in Cincinnati, therefore, has to be understood as a subset of the story of Cincinnati Jewry and of the city of Cincinnati.

Indeed, the Queen City was an important intellectual center for innovations in the medical field, and as this book will document, the history of the Cincinnati Jewish community and the medical profession intersect on a number of levels. While most people know the story of Albert Sabin, developer of the oral polio vaccine, the long and full story of the contributions of Cincinnati Jewry and the Jewish Hospital to the community as a whole have yet to be told in any detail. In addition to the fields of research on disease prevention, members of the Cincinnati Jewish community were prominent in developing medical education, new treatments for cancer and the introduction of new psychological treatments for children.

The Jewish Hospital building in 2015—now part of the University of Cincinnati Med system. *Photo by author.*

The book follows the story of the Jewish Hospital in a chronological order. At the end of each chapter, readers will find brief sketches of the medical history of the region (such as in the first chapter) and biographical sketches of some of the prominent Cincinnati Jews in medicine. This study makes no claims to be a comprehensive history of Jewish medicine in the Queen City. Rather, by focusing on the geographic epicenter of Jewish Hospital, Cincinnati General Hospital and the University of Cincinnati Medical School, it seeks to reveal how the Jewish community responded to the medical challenges of a city during a period of rapid social and economic change.

The list of people whose help I have called on to the make this project a reality is long, and as with all of my scholarly endeavors, if I have forgotten anyone I sincerely apologize. My first debt is to Steve Marine, now retired as executive director of the Henry R. Winkler Center for the History of Health Professions. In 2007, Steve suggested I take on this project and then gently prodded me through to completion; despite the extra length of time to completion, he has remained supportive. Doris Haag, chief archivist of the Winkler Center, also now retired, did yeoman's service in document retrieval and was always available for a quick discussion. Current archivist Veronica

Buchanan cheerfully helped me with last-minute documents and photo retrieval. The librarians at University of Cincinnati Clermont, my academic home, were skillful and patient in answering questions, finding citations and delivering material. The entire University of Cincinnati Library system is made up of dedicated and competent professionals, and it is truly one of the treasures of the university.

My first foray into writing about the history of Cincinnati's Jewish community was done in conjunction with John Fine. Sadly, John died not long after our 2007 book, *The Jews of Cincinnati*, was published. John was stricken with polio when he was nine and confined for the rest of his life to a wheelchair, something he refused to allow to hinder his enthusiasm for scholarship. John was an indefatigable personality, and I am sad that he was not able to work on this project with me, as he would have made it a better book and almost certainly would have ensured that we finished at a faster pace. Saul Benison, wise teacher, benefactor and master of humor, first got me interested in medical history and also, incidentally, provided the connection to Steve Marine; I think it is fair to say that this project would also not exist were it not for Saul. My dissertation adviser, Dr. Henry R. Winkler, was always a model scholar and an extraordinarily decent human being. I miss his intellectual and emotional support. Twenty years, almost to the day, after defending my dissertation, he was present when I gave the 2012 Cecil Stryker Lecture on the history of Jewish Hospital and Jews and medicine in Cincinnati, the talk that led to this book. If I have any regrets, it is that John, Saul and Henry died before I completed this project. It is to these three teachers, friends and mentors that I dedicate this book.

I remain fortunate above all in friends and colleagues. Jim Westheider has encouraged me and let me draw on his knowledge of Cincinnati history since we first met as graduate students in 1986. Jim has been one of the pillars of my intellectual life, and I now have the added bonus of teaching with him at UC Clermont. Whenever I was stuck on a topic, a conversation with Jim usually cleared the blockade and improved my thinking. Robert Miller, another old friend from graduate school I was able to lure to teach at UC Clermont, facilitated my contact with The History Press. I count myself fortunate that after nearly thirty years of friendship, we all still have things to talk and write about.

Colleagues at UC Clermont who also provided encouragement and acted as sounding boards for my harebrained ideas include Greg Loving, Phoebe Reeves, Kim Jacobs-Beck and Wilhelm Kossenjans. John Brolley of UC Judaic Studies read drafts of the chapters and prevented me from serious grammatical errors, as well as encouraged me to believe that the project had the potential to be interesting to others. Thanks also to the rest of the Judaic Studies department for the group discussion in translating the Hebrew phrase on the donor tables discussed in the first chapter.

Kevin Proffitt and the staff of the Jacob Rader Marcus Center of the American Jewish Archives provided access to documents and pictures at a critical time. The Public Library of Cincinnati and Hamilton County has an outstanding collection and had already digitized the Sanborn Fire Maps by the time I began my research, saving me a lot of time and trouble. Pictures of the original Jewish Hospital building on Burnet Avenue, along with some other interesting images on the history of the Hospital, were located in the Cincinnati Historical Society collection.

Jerry Emmert has cared for the physical infrastructure of the old Jewish Hospital building on Burnet Avenue for a long time. Jerry first showed me the stone tablets now housed in the basement and then provided access so I could take some pictures on very short notice; it is caretakers such as Jerry who are the friends of preservationists. Brian Jaffee at the Jewish Foundation of Cincinnati has been supportive and cheerful, despite the delays in getting this project finished. At the Mercy Health Foundation, Roger LaGreca helped with the final push to completion, and a special shout-out also goes to Ann Marie Welty for all her cheerful efforts on my behalf. Krista Slavicek of The History Press was extremely patient and cheerful, an ideal commissioning editor to work with.

My greatest debt is to my wife, Claire Krome, who shares my love of history and supports me when I am working long hours to finish a project. I am grateful and lucky to have a great family: my stepchildren, Karen and Chris, along with grandchildren Steven, Savannah, Samantha, Serenity, Kaarena and Phoenix, keep life interesting. My sister-in-law, Cathy Helfrich, and her son, Nick, pretend to be interested in what I am doing, a good and useful trait. Meanwhile, my two brothers-in-law, Jim and Tim McKeown, and their families remind me that satire is the key to keeping life in perspective. Family reminds me that at the end of the day, it is all about taking care of those you love, as well as sometimes letting them take care of you.

Chapter 1

THE ORIGINS AND EARLY HISTORY OF THE JEWISH HOSPITAL, 1850–1890

In the middle decades of the nineteenth century, Cincinnati was home to the third-largest Jewish communities in the United States, after Philadelphia and New York City. Cincinnati, also known as the Queen City of the West, was the jumping-off point for much of the trade that linked the Mississippi Valley with the northwestern United States, especially after the completion of the Miami Canal and Erie Canal in 1845. As such, the city not only was home to extensive merchant firms but also was a hub for construction—especially riverboats—as well as a center for the processing of food products such as pork, giving the city its other nickname: Porkopolis.

It was in such a mercantile climate that the first Jewish settlers came to Cincinnati and established the institutional framework of a community in the early decades of the nineteenth century. The first Jewish organization in Cincinnati was the burial society; this was followed by the chartering of the first synagogue, K.K. Bene Israel (in 1824), along with the earliest Jewish schools. In European communities, whether they be the eastern European *shtetls* or the central European ghettos, communal institutions such as synagogues, burial societies or schools or the care of the sick and indigent were run by established communal authorities such as rabbis. In this context, communal authorities also had enforcement powers granted by state and local governments, and thus in the Old World the Jewish establishment could levy de facto taxes on the Jewish community to pay for its institutions.

In the United States, however, no such power existed either to enforce religious conformity or levy taxes to support Jewish institutions. Here, all religion, whether tied to ethnicity or religious authorities such as the papacy, was voluntary; indeed it was only the desire of the individual to be a member of a community that defined the level of involvement. So while some older models of philanthropy could serve as inspiration, the voluntary nature of communal life required American Jews to develop new methods of philanthropy and communal organization that could support Jewish institutional life. It was out of this new reality that the Jewish Hospital of Cincinnati would be born.

ORIGINS: FIRST THERE WAS THE IDEA

The year 1854 is the generally accepted date for the foundation of the Jewish Hospital. In fact, this year only became the accepted origin date in the 1920s, when it was utilized as a reference point as part of a fundraising drive by the Jewish Hospital. Since the earliest formal minutes of the board of trustees—or board of control, as it was originally known—date from the 1880s, establishing the exact chronology of the Hospital's founding is tricky. As Cincinnati did not have a Jewish newspaper until 1854, when the *Israelite* (later renamed the *American Israelite*) was founded by Rabbi Isaac Mayer Wise, it is difficult to find contemporaneous information on the process of establishing the Hospital. To date, no information has been located in local synagogue records, and in fact, the earliest information on the origins of Cincinnati's Jewish Hospital comes from Jewish periodicals outside Cincinnati.

Interestingly, it was the Philadelphia Jewish newspaper the *Occident*, edited by Isaac Lesser, that contains the earliest known references to the origins of the Jewish Hospital. In an 1850 editorial, Lesser wrote:

> *We are highly pleased to learn that the Israelites of this flourishing city [Cincinnati] have made a commencement in the establishment of a Jewish Hospital. Several instances have occurred where deceased persons belonging to our persuasion had died in the general hospitals, and been buried without the presence or knowledge even of the Jews, without a brother or a sister in faith being present to repeat a prayer or to do the least office of kindness and affection. This at length roused the sensibilities of several rightly feeling men, and, as we understand, Mr. Hyman Moses and Mr. M.E. Moehring undertook to make collection sufficient to furnish a house with the necessary articles, and having succeeded in this, the hospital has*

been opened forthwith, by placing in it a superintendent, who if necessary, is authorized to get assistances to aid him in his labours.

The article goes on to identify the superintendent as Dr. Henry M. Cohen and describes the subscription process whereby the Jews of Cincinnati contributed money to pay for the hospital. Of key interest is the justification for establishing a Jewish hospital:

> [T]*here are many Israelites all around Cincinnati, many living in the country, and this without friends or family around them, who when they are taken sick have to seek the large city…and hitherto, they had to go to the general infirmaries, because they could obtain no Jewish boarding-house which could render them assistance, even by paying for it.*

Lesser continued, noting that it was both the common Jewish desire to aid the suffering—referring to the tradition of *tzedakah* (charity)—as well as the need of the populace for a "comforting place." To Lesser, the justification for a Jewish hospital was to create a place of safety for the sick and indigent, surrounded by those who shared his/her religious proclivities (emphasis original):

> [A]*nd he must ardently desire not to have his hours of illness embittered by the appeals of those who prowl about sanitary establishments, and omit no opportunity to preach their unwelcome doctrines to all ears, in season and out of season; not to mention the dread which the consciousness invalid must feel of being tampered with in moments of unconsciousness,* as there are zealots who would not hesitate to baptize, as they call it, a Jew or heretic, or infidel, in extremis, *so as to prepare his soul for heaven, even if he be entirely unaware of the act or ceremony which is performed on him.*

Lesser ended his article with a prayer that the "experiment just commenced in Cincinnati may not fail" and that other Jewish communities will follow the Queen City's example.

Now, there are several things of interest in this column, the first of which is the publication date of 1850. This is four years prior to the latter accepted date for the founding of the Jewish Hospital, while the Cincinnati *Williams City Directory* makes its first reference to the Jewish Hospital as being founded in 1850. An article in the second issue of the Cincinnati Jewish newspaper the *Israelite* also refers to an earlier date:

Among the many charitable Jewish institutions established in Cincinnati, the present hospital is the most important, affording as it does, an asylum for the destitute and sick of our community. This institution which was founded in July 1850 owes its origins to the indefatigable zeal of Mr. Hyman Moses, assisted by Messers Joseph Alexander and M.E. Mochring.

Why the discrepancy in the dates? One explanation lies in the utilization of anniversaries by the later administration. In the early twentieth century, the Jewish Hospital collated its own version of its history as part of a fundraising effort and established 1854, the formal incorporation of the Jewish Hospital Association, as the foundation date. Before the establishment of the first purpose-built hospital, provisions were being made to support the sick within the community at a different location, on Betts Street, which was owned by a private individual. Later historians often mistake the incorporation of the association with the opening of the Hospital building, and as such, the foundation date and the creation of a specialized facility were conflated. Perhaps of greater importance than the question of when the physical structure, or indeed the association, was founded is the realization that the *idea* of a Jewish hospital and the formation of an association with a board of trustees predated the dedication of a formal building.

Further proof of the earlier date is found in a reference in the published minutes of the Hospital's board that appeared in the *Israelite* in March 1866. At that time, the Hospital building was being upgraded and a reference was made to the institution being founded in 1849, but that Hospital remained a "small concern" until the noted American Jewish philanthropist Judah Touro of New Orleans gave a $500 gift to expand the facility.

The earliest known records of the Jewish Hospital itself date from a meeting on December 17, 1854. At this incorporation meeting, seven resolutions were passed. Six dealt with the name/title of the organization and its governance, and only the second point dealt with a justification for the establishment of the Jewish Hospital: "That the object of said society shall be for the purpose of alleviating the indigent poor sick of the Jewish faith."

An analysis of the remaining resolutions provides important insight into the organization and purpose of the Hospital. The first point to consider is the absence of any mention of a permanent medical staff. In the twentieth century, Jewish hospitals were established in large cities such as New York, Philadelphia and Chicago in part because Jewish doctors were being denied a place to practice in existing institutions. Such a justification is missing from the rationale for a Jewish Hospital in Cincinnati in the mid-nineteenth century because the goal of the Hospital was not the cure of the sick.

In this early phase of its history, the Hospital was more akin to a hospice and old-age home and also provided temporary lodging for the sick and the indigent. The Jewish Hospital was not identified as a place of healing for several decades; indeed, according to an early twentieth-century recollection, only one room of the building was "set aside for the care of the sick." The focus on indigent care exclusive of healing was very common for the mid-nineteenth century, and the general public did not automatically associate hospitals with surgery or treatment per se. Hospitals in this era were highly specialized—fever hospitals,

An early report (1855) of the Jewish Hospital Association, published in Cincinnati's *Israelite* (later *American Israelite*).

CINCINNATI, Sept. 24th 1855.

TO THE REV. DR. WISE:

Dear Sir,—I beg leave to enclose herewith a statement showing the standing of the Hospital which together with some remarks on the subject you will be kind enough, according to the promises of the Rev. Dr. Lilienthal, to give space in your valuable paper, the *Israelite*. Very respectfully, Yours,

JACOB ELSAS.

Report of the Jewish Hospital of Cincinnati from the 26th October 1854 up to Sept. 30th 1855.

Admitted into the Hospital 65 patients.

Expenses for Boarding, &c.	$588	60
Salary " Stewart	250	00
Salary " Doctor	120	00
Bills " Medicines, &c.	100	00
House rent and interests on back payment due on this property	250	00
Repairs and sundry expenses	75	00
	$1,383	60

Received, quarterly dues from members.

From July to September 1854	$226 50	00
" October to December	222	00
" January to March 1855	236	25
" April to June	261	25
	$946	00
Off ten per cent for collection	94	60
	$851	50

The friends of the above institute must certainly see, that something substantial and energetical must be done, and forthwith, that the Hospital sink not under the burden of a heavy debt. God has blessed you with wealth, please come up to the mark and tell in plain words, how many dollars and cents—you have to spare and are willing to contribute towards the Hospital. There is no time now for excuses, money, and money and again money is wanted. Come up and pay.

Ed. Is.

This is believed to be the only known picture of the first Jewish Hospital on Betts Street, although some sources misidentify it as being the hospital on Third and Baum Streets. *Courtesy Jacob Rader Marcus Center of the American Jewish Archives.*

lunatic hospitals, maternity hospitals, orphan hospitals—while many religious hospitals, such as those run by Catholic institutions, placed their emphasis not on curative care but on dying properly.

In the founding of the Jewish Hospital, prominent and not so prominent members of the community each contributed to a subscription, usually up to five dollars per year. They were unlikely to ever need the services of the Hospital, as the emphasis was on the poor and indigent—people who could afford it were treated in their homes. The involvement in a charitable association was tied to a long Jewish tradition that well-off members of the community had an obligation to help those less fortunate. The subscription fee made the donor a part of the Jewish Hospital Association, which included the right (or obligation) to help set policy and administer the institution.

The association was run by lay leaders, some with no medical background, who were usually the self-appointed stewards of communal institutions. This fit with nineteenth-century notions of philanthropy, which were very paternalistic. Well into the twentieth century, a large percentage of the board of the Jewish Hospital was composed of the business elite of Cincinnati's Jewish community—a self-perpetuating clique of men that expressed its civic pride and social prestige by serving as steward of communal institutions that served the spiritual and physical well-being of the population.

LOCATION: THE POOR EAST SIDE (BUT WITH A GREAT VIEW)

Before discussing the evolution of the Jewish Hospital during the first half century of its existence, we need to consider the significance of the decision to locate the Hospital on the eastern side of the city. In almost all industrial cities in the western world, the east end that was the home of the working classes and poor. In the twentieth century, however, Cincinnati was unique in that it was the west end of the city that became the home of the working classes.

Only one photo said to be of the original hospital building is known to exist, although there is some controversy over whether it is the building on Betts Street or the second location. The Jewish Hospital building was situated near the corner of Third and Baum Streets, which sits at the bottom of the Cincinnati neighborhood known as Mount Adams. Third and Baum, however, was not part of that neighborhood but rather is located in what is known today as the Historic East End of Cincinnati. In the mid-nineteenth century, this area sat on the periphery of the city limits and was part of an industrial region that served the burgeoning riverboat and railroad network. While today the area between the base of Mount Adams and outskirts of the downtown business districts is dominated by parking lots and the Interstate 71/Interstate 471 highway network, in 1854 the Hospital was, in fact, close to the African American neighborhood known as "Little Africa."

Indeed, the Jewish Hospital was three blocks from the Little Miami Rail Road Depot, as well as the Ohio River and a construction site for riverboats. Interestingly, the Old Marine Hospital, which served the merchant marine community, was right across the street from the Jewish Hospital. Like the Jewish Hospital, the Marine Hospital was a philanthropic institution; unlike the Jewish Hospital, however, the Marine

The second location of the Jewish Hospital, dedicated in 1866, had a view of downtown and the riverfront; however, no trace of the structure remains. *Photo by author.*

Hospital was a federally chartered institution, one of more than a dozen in the United States chartered in the nineteenth century. The Cincinnati location was founded sometime after the great cholera epidemics of 1832, around the same time as the institution in St. Louis was built; its mission was to serve the medical needs of sailors, who were the lifeblood of the nation's commerce in the nineteenth century.

The location of the Jewish Hospital was on the opposite side of the city from the major institutions of the Cincinnati Jewish community, such as the Chestnut Street Cemetery and the major synagogues. The geographic pattern strongly suggests that while the Cincinnati Jewish community felt an obligation to support the poor and indigent, it nonetheless did not necessarily want to be in proximity to them. The location, just over a mile from one of Cincinnati's first permanent synagogue buildings near the modern intersection of Walnut and Seventh Street, probably was also relatively inexpensive to purchase.

The Old Marine Hospital sat right across the street from the Jewish Hospital on Third and Baum Streets. Nothing remains of this structure.

No trace of the two hospitals remains today, and indeed, the corner of Third and Baum no longer exists, destroyed by the post-1945 construction of the highway system. Third Street is now a one-way boulevard going west, and in order to reach Baum Street, you must either travel up through Mount Adams and south or cross to the East End and double back north. Although the neighborhood is undergoing gentrification, you can get a sense of what it felt like to a nineteenth-century denizen of the Hospital by standing at the spot where the two buildings once stood.

THE JEWISH HOSPITAL:
EARLY YEARS OF OPERATION

The original Jewish Hospital was described (in 1866) as a "double three story house on an elevation framed in Dayton stone and iron rails." The first floor contained offices and one small room that could be utilized as a synagogue. The Hospital's capacity was sixteen patients/residents on the second floor, while the third floor was apparently for storage. Several early twentieth-century sources listed the construction cost at about $40,000.

It is difficult to reconstruct the activities of the Jewish Hospital during the first three decades of its operational life. The extant board minutes only date from 1887, and prior to that point, the only major data available were reports of the annual meeting, which were published in the *Israelite*. Still, the annual reports do provide a snapshot of issues facing the hospital. For example, in September 1855, only a year after formal incorporation, the Hospital was listed as serving sixty-five patients—although given the size of the institution certainly not all at the same time—and having two salaried staff: a steward, paid $250 per year, and a doctor, paid $120 per year. The varied amounts probably reflected their importance to the running of the hospital. Salary, medicine and operating expenses came to $1,383, while the amount brought in via subscription and donation was only $851.50. Thus we see that from its very beginning the institution struggled with funding. After detailing the breakdown of costs and income, Jacob Elsas, president of the board of control, wrote:

> *The friends of the above institution must certainly see that something substantial and energetical* [sic] *must be done and forthwith that the Hospital not sink under the burden of heavy debt. God has blessed you with wealth, please come up to the mark and tell in plain words how many dollars and cents you have to spare and are willing to contribute towards the Hospital. There is no time now for excuses, money and money and money again is wanted. Come up and pay.*

As stated earlier, the financial needs of running a Jewish communal institution—whether it be a synagogue, burial society, school or hospital—in nineteenth-century America was dependent on voluntary membership in these institutions. A study of such institutions, therefore, can help the student of history gauge everything from communal solidarity to economic vibrancy. Interestingly, the monetary crisis that was identified in the earliest reports from the Jewish Hospital remained a consistent challenge for the institution throughout its existence and finds echoes in other communal organizations.

We can glean something about the process of funding the Hospital, and what the institution meant to the city of Cincinnati, from a fascinating set of physical artifacts that date from the Hospital's early era. Sometime in the late nineteenth or early twentieth century, the Hospital Association carved the names of the major donors, starting with Judah Touro, into a set of marble tablets. These tablets once flanked the entryway of the second

The first of a series of memorial tablets listing the earliest donors to the Jewish Hospital. Judah Touro was a resident of New Orleans and an active philanthropist to Jewish causes. *Photo by author.*

Hospital building (see second chapter for details of the second building) until they were taken down during renovations after World War II.

Next to each name is the amount of their gifts, which vary between $5,000 (from Touro) and $100 donations from a variety of individuals; it is, however, the list of names that is particularly interesting. In addition to familiar names of the Cincinnati Jewish community, such as Workum, Mack, Fleischmann, Strauss, Lilienthal and Friedman, there are quite a few non-Jews. As Don Heinrich Tolzmann, the leading authority on Cincinnati's German heritage, once remarked upon reading a list of the names, "The tablets are a who's who of Cincinnati German families." For example, the famous beer brewer Christian Moerlein donated $250 to the Jewish Hospital Association.

It is also interesting that at the top of each tablet is a Hebrew inscription paraphrased from Psalm 103:14, which reads (in translation): "Remember that we are Dust." (The original phrase from Psalm 103:14 is, "For he knoweth our frame he remembers that we are dust.") The phrase is not commonly associated with philanthropic bequests, at least in Jewish institutions. It

זכר כי עפר אנחנו

BEQUESTS

SOPHIE STRAUSS	500
FANNIE FRIEDMAN	100
EMANUEL M. MOERS	100
ALEXANDER ASSUR	200
A. J. FRIEDLANDER	500
JEPTHA L. & EZEKIEL L. WORKUM	5000
MINNA FECHHEIMER	100
CHRISTIAN MOERLEIN	250
MATHILDA WEIL	100
JOSEPH EISEMAN	1000
PHILIP TROUNSTINE	100
CHARLES FLEISCHMAN	1000

The memorial tablets indicate that non-Jews also donated to the Jewish Hospital. Christian Moerlein was a prominent Cincinnati brewer. *Photo by author.*

was, however, commonly cited by Catholic charities in the same period. Considering that Cincinnati was a heavily German Catholic city, especially in this period, and that the leadership of the Cincinnati Jewish community was predominately German Jewish, the confluence of the two groups in supporting the Hospital should not be too surprising.

A further illustration of the role of the Jewish Hospital as a communal institution can be gleaned by an analysis of a short news item from Isaac Mayer Wise's *Israelite* of April 24, 1890:

The top of the tablets contain a Hebrew inscription paraphrased from Psalm 103:14 that reads, "Remember that we are dust." *Photo by author.*

A Catholic priest administered the last sacrament to a Roman Catholic patient last Saturday in the Jewish Hospital in Cincinnati. The patient died, and, of course, was buried as a Catholic. This is not wonderful, as many Israelites died in Catholic hospitals and were buried according to Jewish rites. Remarkable in this case is that the patient, a lady of wealth, preferred the Jewish hospital, and that the priest went to her to that place. The fact is that the Jewish hospital is now an excellently managed institution, with all modern improvements, in a very fine location; and the Catholic priesthood in Cincinnati is much more liberal than it is in smaller places.

This story in Cincinnati's Jewish newspaper provides several important insights into the history of the Jewish Hospital of Cincinnati. The first is that despite the sectarian name of the hospital from a very early stage, it was open to all regardless of race or creed. The second point, concerning the commentary "excellently managed institution with all modern improvements," is, we shall see, a statement about the new building, geographic location and organization of the Jewish Hospital, which started downtown but was in the process of migrating (along with the Jewish community it served). Indeed, by

1890 the Jewish Hospital had evolved from an ad hoc organization and was quickly developing into what came to be known as a "scientifically" managed establishment. By the end of the nineteenth century, the Jewish Hospital was not only a prominent communal institution run by Cincinnati's Jewish economic and social elite but also a Cincinnati community institution.

CINCINNATI'S MEDICAL HISTORY

The story of the Jewish Hospital reveals that Cincinnati has a long and rich medical history. In addition to the Jewish and Marine Hospitals, Cincinnati had at least at least half a dozen hospitals by the end of the Civil War. Many of these hospitals have long and storied histories. For example, the Cincinnati Commercial and Lunatic Asylum, built in the 1820s and originally located between Plum and Central Avenue, was acquired by the city in 1861. Its name was changed to the Commercial Hospital, and in 1868, its name was changed again, to Cincinnati Hospital. In the early twentieth century, the name was changed yet again, to Cincinnati General Hospital, and it was moved to its current location near the University of Cincinnati. It is now UC Medical.

Some of the earliest physicians to practice in the Queen City were military surgeons attached to the various U.S. Army units stationed in the area. The most famous medical pioneer was Daniel Drake. Drake was not Jewish, yet he played an important role in establishing a number of the institutions that figure prominently in the story of Jews and medicine in Cincinnati. Drake was one of the founders of the Medical College of Ohio, which in 1896 became the Medical Department of the University of Cincinnati, an institution that, as we shall see, developed a close relationship to the Jewish Hospital. A number of staff physicians at the Jewish Hospital also taught at the Medical School, while graduates of the medical school served as interns and residents at the Jewish Hospital.

We know little about the earliest physicians to work at the Jewish Hospital; however, by the early twentieth century, biographical and professional information had become more plentiful. Without further information on the doctors who attended the residents of the Jewish Hospital in this earlier era, we cannot even speculate as to their specific training or professional trajectory.

Chapter 2

THE MOVE TO PILL HILL AND THE EVOLUTION OF JEWS AND MEDICINE IN CINCINNATI, 1890–1922

On March 30, 1890, the new building of the Jewish Hospital was dedicated on Burnet Avenue, on the border between the neighborhoods of Mount Auburn and Avondale. While this ten-block area of Cincinnati eventually became known as "Pill Hill" for the confluence of medical establishments, in 1890 the Jewish Hospital stood nearly alone. The dedication ceremony brought together the philanthropic and religious leadership of the Cincinnati Jewish community: the opening prayer was led by Dr. Isaac Mayer Wise, the rabbi of K.K. Bene Jeshurun (now Wise Center) and also the founder and president of the Hebrew Union College, the rabbinical seminary for Reform Judaism. The first address was given by Wise's protégé, Dr. David Philipson, who served as rabbi of the K.K. Bene Israel Congregation (now known as Rockdale Temple) and who apparently was speaking on behalf of the Cincinnati Jewish community. Julius Freiberg, the head of the building committee, presented the key to the new building to the Jewish Hospital Association president, James Lowman. The Freiberg family included several prominent physicians in the twentieth century, one of whom even consulted with Franklin Delano Roosevelt in the late 1920s on treatments for polio sufferers. The head of the medical staff, Joseph Ransohoff, who was the patriarch of a medical dynasty, represented the Hospital's physicians on the podium.

Another dedication for the Hospital occurred on October 22, 1922. This event marked the opening of a major expansion to the physical infrastructure

JEWISH HOSPITAL,

BURNET AVENUE, AVONDALE.

··DEDICATION,··

MARCH 30, 1890, at 2 o'clock P. M.

✠ PROGRAMME. ✠

1. PRAYER, - - - - DR. I. M. WISE

2. DELIVERY OF KEY BY CHAIRMAN OF BUILDING
   COMMITTEE, - - JULIUS FREIBERG

3. ACCEPTANCE OF KEY BY THE PRESIDENT, JAMES LOWMAN

4. ADDRESS, - - - DR. DAVID PHILLIPSON

5. ADDRESS IN BEHALF OF THE MEDICAL STAFF
   BY THE DEAN, - - DR. JOS. RANSOHOFF

6. BENEDICTION, - - DR. DAVID DAVIDSON

BLOCH PRINTING CO.

The dedication ceremony of the Burnet Avenue building in 1890 featured the leadership of Cincinnati's religious and philanthropic community.

The Jewish Hospital on Burnet Avenue circa 1890, shortly after it was opened. *Courtesy Cincinnati Historical Society.*

of the Jewish Hospital, specifically the building of a maternity ward. The cast of characters had changed somewhat in more than three decades: David Philipson, now an elder statesman of the Cincinnati Jewish community, was on the agenda. There was, however, a new board president, Samuel Strauss, representing the Hospital. Meanwhile, Dr. Sigmar Stark, a junior doctor in 1890, was now head of the medical staff and spoke for the physicians. Of particular interest was the presence on the program of George Carroll, the mayor of Cincinnati, for no representative of the city government had officially been part of the 1890 event.

While both occasions were probably similar—long speeches combined with the usual appeals to join and participate in the noble endeavor of supporting the Hospital (i.e., give money)—between the building of a new Hospital in 1890 and the dedication of its expansion in 1922, the nature of hospital organization and medical care had changed. Indeed, the structure and location of the Cincinnati Jewish community had undergone a transformation as well. The shifts in the city and its Jewish

Cincinnati, Ohio. October 22, 1922.

PROGRAM

Laying of the Corner Stone of the
Jewish Hospital.

1. Prayer...................... Rabbi David Philipson.

2. Address...................... Mr. Samuel Straus, President
The Jewish Hospital

3. Address...................... Hon. George Carrol
Mayor of Cincinnati.

4. Address...................... Dr. Sigmar Stark
Dean of Medical Staff.

5. Sealing up of Copper Box containing:

Names of Board of Trustees.
Names of Building Committee.
Names of Medical Staff.
Names of Hospital Faculty.
Names of Architect and Builders.
Training School for Nurses and
heads of Departments.
History of the Jewish Hospital
by Louis Cooper Levy, Superintendent.
Photograph of Mrs. Maurice J. Freiberg,
in whose memory the building was erected.
Photograph of the Jewish Hospital as it
appears today.
Photograph of the New Hospital.

Dedication program from the 1922 expansion of the maternity wing, which featured the religious and civic leaders of the Jewish community along with the mayor of Cincinnati.

community were reflected in the physical and philosophical place of the Jewish Hospital within the wider Cincinnati community. In fact, it was during this period, usually defined as the Progressive Era, that the physical structure and practices of the Jewish Hospital moved from an ad hoc administrative system to modern management, while the practice of medicine also entered the modern age.

HISTORICAL CONTEXT:
CHANGES IN THE CINCINNATI JEWISH COMMUNITY

The city of Cincinnati had undergone major transformation since 1850. For example, its position as the gateway to western commerce was challenged by the spread of railroads, while the rise of Chicago as a production center for beef and pork meant that Cincinnati's dominance as America's Porkopolis was fading. Yet the city remained an important transportation and industrial hub. Indeed, the growth of industrialization had led to an expansion of Cincinnati's population after 1880, which like the rest of the United States meant an increase in the number of immigrants from eastern Europe. For Cincinnati's Jewish community, which was dominated by German Jewish immigrants, this meant learning to live with a number of new arrivals who changed its demographic and religious profile. The new immigrants spoke a different language (Yiddish) than the established community, while their religious practices were often more traditional than those of American Reform Judaism, of which Wise and Philipson were prominent proponents, and which dominated Cincinnati's communal affairs. The result was that in the last decades of the nineteenth and first years of the twentieth centuries, the religious unity of Cincinnati Jewry, tenuous as it had been, was shattered as new congregations and new voices in communal affairs proliferated.

In addition to the increased diversity of religious practice, the geographic focus of Cincinnati Jewry was being transformed. When the Jewish Hospital was founded in the mid-nineteenth century, it was located in the poor section of the city and yet was still within two square miles of other Jewish communal institutions, such as synagogues and the cemetery. As the Jewish community spread out from downtown, this geographic center was lost. An examination of the location of both synagogues and the addresses of members of the community helps gives a sense of this dispersal. For example, in the early twentieth century, an Orthodox congregation and cemetery was founded in Price Hill, on the western side of town, while some members of the soon-to-be-famous Manischewitz family, whose business interests started in Cincinnati, listed their addresses on Glenway Avenue, which was also on the city's west side and more than seven miles away. Perhaps this is not a great distance by modern standards, but in the pre-automotive era, it was something of a trek.

Meanwhile, the German Jewish population, and those members of the newer immigrants who were reaching middle-class status, began moving out of downtown and into the northern Cincinnati neighborhood called Avondale. Given the dominant position of the old German Jewish elite at the helm of the Jewish Hospital, it is not surprising, therefore, that when looking for a new location they chose one in physical proximity to where their part of the community was migrating.

The choice of the Burnet Avenue location for the new facility, however, cannot be interpreted merely as the result of the biases of the board of trustees. The location also reflects how attitudes toward medicine, and toward the activities of the hospital, had begun to change in the mere thirty years since the founding of the association.

CHANGES IN AMERICAN MEDICINE AND THE ROLE OF THE HOSPITAL

As we saw in the first chapter, when the Jewish Hospital was founded in the mid-nineteenth century, it served as both a refuge for the sick and the elderly indigent and as a hospice. By the late nineteenth century, the specialized hospitals that had characterized medical treatment for several generations—fever hospitals, maternity hospitals, foundling hospitals—were shifting into a new pattern. Many of the old-style specialty hospitals began to close down and were replaced by civic institutions, often dubbed general hospitals, as one of the new norms. The general hospital was a publicly funded institution, usually on a city or county level, and as the name implied, it dealt in the treatment of all manner of ailments. The other pole from the civic establishment included sectarian institutions such as Good Samaritan and Christ Hospital (to use two Cincinnati examples), which were sponsored by religious groups. Cincinnati's Jewish Hospital fit somewhere between these two poles; while it was not sponsored and run by local government, it was (to use a modern term) a nonsectarian Jewish institution, not being run by any one denomination or specific group within the Jewish community. Interestingly, as we shall see, the Jewish Hospital did not even have a formal hospital rabbi, chapel or a kosher kitchen until well into the twentieth century. Remarkably, the absence of these distinctly Jewish traits was not considered significant in 1890 and only became a source of controversy in the 1930s.

The change in institutional sponsorship and the rise of the general (or public) hospital also reflected changes in how these institutions functioned.

Instead of being viewed solely as hospices and places for aged indigents, hospitals were now regarded as places of treatment. Patients did not go to a hospital with the expectation to die (although that continued to be a reality), but rather for healing. As the function of the hospital changed, the nature of staffing would also change. For example, in its early days, the Jewish Hospital had a full-time steward and a part-time physician. By the beginning of the twentieth century, the functioning of the Jewish Hospital required the presence of multiple physicians, nurses and support staff. Managing this diverse group and maintaining the physical infrastructure soon required a full-time administrator with his own support staff. The increased size and complexity of the staff was matched by an increased sophistication in medical equipment. All of these elements combined to increase the cost of maintaining a hospital.

Concomitant with the changes in hospitals in the late nineteenth century was a transformation in medicine. Prior to the Progressive Era (circa 1890), there was no formal or consistent process to achieve professional status in many fields. Indeed, many professionals in law, medicine, science and engineering were autodidacts and/or self-proclaimed. Progressive Era reforms changed the status of the professional in all fields. A regular system of education and either certification or a university degree were fast becoming the means to identify as a professional. While medical education was often associated with university training, many medical colleges did not have a consistent curriculum for practical training in a hospital setting. The culmination of the desire to promote more consistent and better medical education led to the 1910 publication of the *Flexner Report*, written by Abraham Flexner (incidentally, an American Jew from Louisville) and sponsored by the Carnegie Foundation. Medical schools were advised to tighten admission and graduation requirements, train students in the latest scientific methods and provide practical training in a clinical setting, specifically a hospital. The result was a reduction in the number of medical schools and a smaller and more highly trained pool of physicians that worked in greater cooperation with hospitals. In Cincinnati, the University of Cincinnati Medical School embraced the guidelines of the *Flexner Report*, while the Jewish Hospital became one of the places where medical reform was implemented.

THE WORKINGS OF THE JEWISH HOSPITAL
AND THE MOVE TO PILL HILL

In 1888, the lot on Burnet Avenue and Union Street was purchased for $8,000. While this location was about two and half miles from the old hospital building, it was a world apart in character. Whereas Third and Baum was part of the east end—a poor section of town and close to industrial works and "Little Africa"—the Burnet Avenue location bordered on Mount Auburn and Avondale, two areas that were in the late nineteenth century lightly settled and more bourgeois in character. The move helped establish the region as a desirable location to which the Cincinnati Jewish community could to migrate, as the Hospital was one of the communal institutions, along with synagogues, schools and cemeteries, that served a function in the Jewish life cycle.

The reasons for the decision to move rested on several factors, not all of them medical. By 1888, the activities of the Jewish Hospital had expanded beyond its original remit. For example, where in its first decade of operation the hospital had only a part-time physician, it now required a "Dean of the Medical Staff" to supervise the multiple physicians serving the patients, a role filled initially by Dr. A. Rosenfeld. Although the Jewish Hospital was not yet a place where surgery was routinely performed, the number of and type of patients had expanded. Likewise, medical treatment at the Hospital

This picture of the back of the Jewish Hospital complex in the early twentieth century reveals how sparsely developed the Burnet Avenue area was before the building of the new Cincinnati General Hospital.

had evolved beyond mere palliative care. To give one example, in 1889, Sigmar Stark was appointed the Hospital's obstetrician and gynecologist, indicating the expanding type of care available at the institution. Simply put, the old building had, in the twenty years since its dedication, become inadequate and obsolete for the needs of the community.

By 1887, it had become clear to the board that a new and larger facility was needed. Indeed, one indication of a major change in the philosophy of the association occurred in 1883, when the Jewish Home for Aged and Infirmed was incorporated as a separate entity from the Hospital. Interestingly, the new institution to serve the community's geriatric and disabled population was the first Jewish institution known to be built in the Mount Auburn/Avondale area of Burnet Avenue.

Construction on the new Hospital building began in 1889, and the board's secretary, Louis Kramer, was both optimistic and concerned about the association's future. He wrote in the 1889 annual report:

> *This new Institution will be a credit, not only to our Association but to the entire Jewish community. The Jewish people of this city, however, should be urged to take a more active and material interest in the support of the new Hospital, as it will be necessary to increase the subscription list, and also establish a permanent fund for its maintenance. The opening of this new Hospital will mark a new era in Jewish charities in this community, as we will then have in connection with the new Home, side by side two kindred charities reaching out their generous hands for the relief and comfort of the sick and aged.*

As Kramer's remarks indicated, the dedication of the new Jewish Hospital in 1890 marked not only the expansion of the physical infrastructure but also an increase in the annual costs of running the institution, a challenge that would only accelerate as medical technology continued to develop into the twentieth century and as the number and variety of patients continued to expand.

The dedication speech by Julius Freiberg, who chaired the building committee, reflected traditional Jewish themes of philanthropy and reiterated some of the anxieties expressed by Kramer:

> *"Love they neighbor as thyself," shall be the watchword when no other weapon shall be used except kindness and good will; when the sick and tired of life and its burdens shall be cared for and tenderly nursed, and*

when humanity shall be the supreme ruler.... My hope is that our hospital shall never lack support, and that it will be richly endowed by the good and charitable, and that God's blessing may rest upon all who take an interest in it.

The content of the speeches are not revolutionary, and in fact, they echo issues raised in the earliest known statements about the Jewish Hospital. Simply put, it takes a lot of community support to keep such a complex endeavor afloat. Board president Lowman emphasized these points in an address to the association:

With the running of the Hospital on new lines of progressiveness, and with enlarged facilities, the cost and expense of maintaining the same has naturally increased from what it formally was in the old Institution. We were obliged to go in debt in order to finish the Building owing to our inability to dispose of the old Hospital Property. This is now represented by a bonded indebtedness of $15,000, which we hope to reduce by the sale of the old building, but I regret to say that notwithstanding every effort we have not been successful in disposing of same and the prospects for doing so are not very encouraging owing to its bad location and general undesirability.

Certainly by the late nineteenth century, managing the Jewish Hospital had become a complex endeavor. The board minutes give us a sense of how the Jewish Hospital functioned during this era. The board met every month—prior to 1890 at either the home of the president or a local business owned by one of the members and after 1890 at the Hospital itself. Since board members were not part of the day-to-day administration of the hospital, an ad hoc "Visitors Committee" was tasked with checking up on the hospital's activities, and several members of the board were designated to serve every month.

A list of monthly expenses drawn from board records also provides insight into hospital operations. In one month in 1888, for example, a partial list of expenses ran as follows:

Dr. A Rosenfeld	Salary	$30.00
J. Kibitz	Drugs	5.55
Isaac Wise	Marketing	90.89
H & H Lowenstein	Meat	94.31
H. Raustick	Bread	33.06

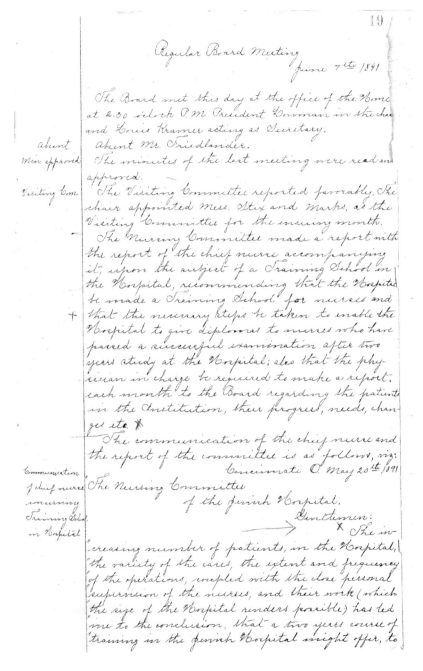

In the 1890s, the minutes of the monthly meetings were still recorded by hand. Every month, the board designated several men to serve as "visitors" to check on the patients and staff of the Hospital.

H. Humminghaack	Milk	17.94
J. Moulden	Beer	33.06
Hamberger & Nearburgh	Groceries	30.07
Cincinnati Ice	Ice	2.90
Faulk A. Kern	Wine	3.00

In addition, monthly charges included such items as coal, tobacco, hosiery and the salaries of nurses. These monthly lists indicate that the hospital obtained some supplies, such as groceries, from multiple sources, while in the case of marketing, the name of Isaac Wise indicates that his newspaper, the *American Israelite*, was the sole venue for publicizing the association's work.

A number of the items purchased every month—such as beer, wine and tobacco—might seem odd to the modern eye. The explanation for their regular supply to the Jewish Hospital must be understood as both a reflection of contemporary medical understanding—for example, tobacco was not generally regarded as a major health hazard—and what later documents reveal was a two-tiered system of patient treatment and accommodation.

By the time the Hospital moved to Pill Hill, it was no longer exclusively a charity organization. In fact, sometime in the previous fifteen years the Hospital had begun accepting paying patients, and those paying for treatment expected such things as alcoholic beverages and tobacco to be available as part of their cure. Indeed, in July 1892, the board set the rate for patients in

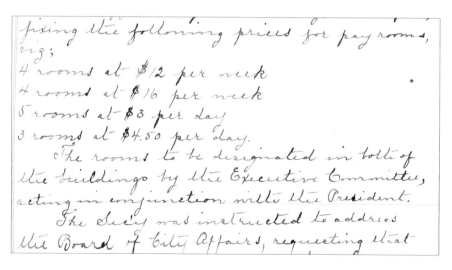

In the late nineteenth century, the Hospital's board of trustees divided the patients in charity and private categories, with the latter being billed set rates for rooms.

one of the paying wards at fifteen dollars per week. It did, however, go on to state that "bandages, medicine, dressing, beer, liquors, were extra." The division of hospital patients into charity and paying categories also provides another dimension to the decision to move from the poor region of town into a more bourgeois neighborhood such as Mount Auburn.

So, by the time the new Hospital was dedicated, its operations had expanded from palliative treatment to active care on a variety of fronts, such as obstetrics, with a diversity of patients who could expect a level of service based on their socioeconomic status. In this context, the Jewish Hospital began to resemble the general hospital model discussed earlier. A growing medical staff was matched by an increased need for nurses, and indeed, in 1890, the board took two steps to meet this need: the promulgation of a set of "Rules for Nurses," and the establishment of a school to train nurses specifically for the Jewish Hospital.

The Establishment of a Nursing School

The parameters of managing the nursing staff were initially set at a board meeting on March 20, 1890. The first step was the establishment of the position of superintendent, who was tasked with "supervising and control of all nursing and other females employed in the Hospital." In addition, the superintendent was to administer daily activities such as scheduling, as well as set rules and regulations for the staff, subject to the approval of a Committee on Nursing established by the board. At the same meeting, the board approved seventeen "Rules for Nurses," summarized as follows:

1. The chief nurse or superintendent was to be in charge of all the nursing staff and handled scheduling and discipline.
2. A graduate nurse was to be in charge of each department, and her orders must be "strictly and respectfully obeyed."
3. All nurses were expected to remain standing when speaking to a physician and while on ward duty.
4. Nurses were to treat patients with respect and not to argue with them.
5. Nurses were not to perform any outside work while on duty.
6. Nurses were to return to their quarters when their shift ends.
7. No friends were allowed to visit while a nurse is on duty.
8. All nurses were to wear uniforms without decoration.

9. Nurses were to have access to laundry facilities and, in fact, were required to wash their uniforms a certain number of times per week,

10. When sick and unable to work their shifts, nurses were to inform the superintendent as soon as possible.

11. No food was allowed in the nurses' dormitory.

12. Nurses on night shift were to be provided with meals but had to remain in their wards while eating.

13. Nurses were not allowed to exchange furniture between their dorm rooms.

14. Nurses not on night shift had a 10:00 p.m. curfew.

15. While the chambermaids cleaned the floors and bathrooms, the nurses were to make their own beds.

16. Nurses were required to maintain personal hygiene but were also enjoined not to waste water or discard "any solid substances into basins."

17. Nurses were to observe the regular meal schedule.

Only the second rule makes reference to a professionalization of the nursing staff, mandating that a "graduate nurse" must be in charge of each department. Six of the rules specifically relate to deportment and behavior; for example, in the third rule nurses are instructed not to "laugh loudly when passing through the corridors" (one assumes that the physicians could guffaw all they wanted), in addition to the requirement that they should remain standing when speaking to a doctor. The other nine rules deal with conduct issues such as curfew, clothing, cleanliness of quarters and respect for Hospital property.

There are several important points that need to be considered when examining these "Rules for Nurses." First, they are obviously an example of a late American Victorian sense of gender roles and propriety, as well as being an example of what we today would regard as a patronizing attitude toward female staff. Yet the rules might also reveal some of the anxieties of the leadership as they prepared to dedicate the new Hospital building, which occurred ten days after the board approved these regulations. Simply put, by 1890 the live-in staff of the Hospital, which included not only nurses but also chambermaids, had grown dramatically. It is likely that their quarters took up a significant amount of space in the new Hospital building, at a time when the hospital was expanding its operation among paying clients. So at least part of the anxiety expressed at the dedication just over a week later might have been the realization among the members of the board of trustees that their facility was already running short of room and that they would shortly have to expand the infrastructure yet again. Significantly, one of the major projects undertaken by the Jewish Hospital a decade later was the building of a nurses' dormitory, which, as it turned out, also included classroom space.

Initially, most of the Jewish Hospital's nursing staff were graduates of the City Hospital (later Cincinnati General Hospital) program. Mary Hamer Greenwood, superintendent of the nurses, argued that the Jewish Hospital needed to establish its own nursing school. As she wrote the board:

> *The increasing number of patients, in the Hospital, the variety of cases, the extent and frequency of the operations, coupled with the close personal supervision of the nurses, and their work (which the size of the Hospital renders possible) has led me to the conclusion, that a two year course of training in the Jewish Hospital might offer, to the nurses forming the school, advantages equal to those, which they enjoy under the present arrangement* [i.e., studying at the City Hospital].

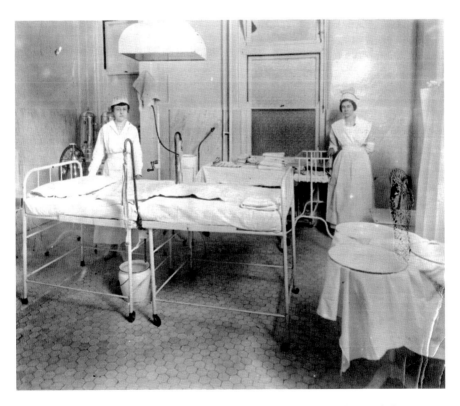

Nurses in one of the treatment rooms at the Jewish Hospital in the early twentieth century. Graduate nurses were considered essential to the smooth running of the Hospital.

Greenwood concluded by stressing the growing reputation of the Jewish Hospital as a medical center and the need to train and retain skilled nurses. A course of study directed by graduate nurses, with lectures by physicians associated with the Jewish Hospital, would, it was argued, go a long way toward ensuring a cadre of qualified caregivers.

In April 1891, the board accepted the plan that the Jewish Hospital become a training school for nurses, and in December of the same year, it established the bylaws of the school. Initially, nursing students would complete a two-year course of study and practicum. Within a few months, the Jewish Hospital had half a dozen students in residence, and Greenwood reported that she had received sixteen applications, some from as close as Kentucky and others from as far away as Canada. The first class of the Jewish Hospital Nursing School graduated in January 1893. The graduation ceremony was held in the chapel of the Jewish Old Age Home, as the Jewish Hospital had no dedicated space for such events.

In September 1900, the association increased the school program to a three-year curriculum, which, according to the report to the board, placed the school "in accordance with best practices" in the country. The third year was added so nursing students would have time to study subjects such as hospital management, housekeeping and procurement of supplies. It would also enable those students who wished to specialize in specific branches of nursing care to "take appropriate advantages." In that same year, seven students completed their training, the largest class to finish to date.

EXPANSION IN THE EARLY TWENTIETH CENTURY

As the new century dawned, the Jewish Hospital had established a character that would not be substantively revised until the post–World War II era. A few years earlier, in May 1898, the Hospital published its official *Rules and Regulations*. These regulations defined the requirements of membership in the Hospital Association—basic dues were set at $5 per year, and $500 would grant a person a lifetime membership. The board of trustees was drawn from the dues paying members of the association, and throughout the first half of the twentieth century, they remained a self-selecting and self-perpetuating group. To become a board member required nomination by a sitting member and then election by the full membership. Given the amount of time and (almost certainly) personal cost involved in serving on the board, it is likely that volunteers from among the association were rare and were drawn from the wealthy members of the Jewish community.

In the 1950s, an internship system was established to help train future association leaders; however, in this era, no such system of mentorship existed, and volunteers willing to spend the necessary time and money were rare and learned on the job. The structure of the Jewish Hospital Board was very similar to other philanthropic organizations of the day, derived from a sense of obligation on the part of those wealthy members of the community who felt it was their duty to actively serve.

The *Rules and Regulations* defined not only membership in the association but also the running of the Hospital itself. It laid out the table of organization of the physicians, nurses and other employees. It is instructive to look at how the medical staff

REGULATIONS AND RULES

OF THE

JEWISH HOSPITAL

OF

CINCINNATI, OHIO,

CORNER BURNET AVE. AND UNION ST., AVONDALE.

REVISED AND ADOPTED MAY, 1898.

PRESS OF
S. ROSENTHAL & CO., 15–27 WEST SIXTH STREET, CINCINNATI, O.
1898.

The *Rules and Regulations* for the Jewish Hospital, published in 1898, revealed that the association was moving from an ad hoc management to modern managerial procedures.

had grown in a mere decade since the new building was dedicated. For example, in 1900, the following medical specialties were listed:

Surgical
Gynecological
Neurological
Eye
Ear, Nose, Throat
Children
Obstetrical
Dental

REGULATIONS.

ARTICLE I.—*Name.*

This Society shall be known as the JEWISH HOSPITAL ASSOCIATION OF CINCINNATI, O.

ARTICLE II.—*Membership.*

Any person may become a member of this Association upon a petition to be accepted by the Board of Directors.

ARTICLE III.—*Dues of Members.*

SECTION 1. The annual dues shall be five dollars or more, payable semi-annually in advance.

SEC. 2. The petition for membership shall state the amount of dues to be paid by the applicant, and this amount shall be charged to him in semi-annual installments until his resignation has been tendered and accepted, unless changed upon written application to the Board of Directors.

SEC. 3. Any member paying to the Association five hundred dollars shall be declared a life member and he sub-

Close-up of the published *Rules and Regulations* detailing membership requirements; the board was a self-selecting, self-perpetuating group.

In addition to the organization of the Hospital staff, of particular interest is how the Hospital Association dealt with the dual nature of the institution, catering to both paying and charity patients. Not surprisingly, the rules governing charity patients were stricter than those related to the paying customers. Charity patients had more limited visiting hours, were held to sterner discipline in terms of their freedom of movement within the Hospital and in general were treated with the paternalism common among institutions in this era.

Paying or "private" patients, as they were called, had greater rights—for example, extended visiting hours and access to better accommodations, including the adult beverages mentioned earlier. Indeed, a clear hierarchy of service for patients was in place by 1900. In the paying wing, there were four rooms with a weekly rate of $12.00 (about a $1.70 per day), four rooms that cost $16.00 per week (a bit over $2.20 per day) and then five rooms at rate of

The medical staff of the Jewish Hospital in 1905 represented more than a dozen specialized fields.

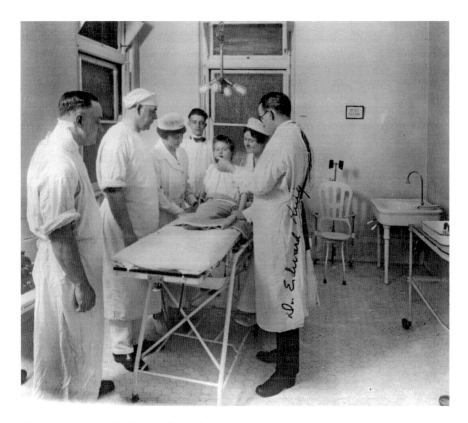

Treatment room of the Jewish Hospital, circa 1916.

$3.00; finally, the most expensive accommodations were three rooms costing $4.50 per day. The cost of service at the Hospital also did not cover physicians or surgical fees, which were to be paid directly to the doctor. Furthermore, if a patient wanted laundry services, that would be an additional fee. The published *Rules* also reiterated the previous regulation that "wines, beer, liquors, etc., (except when ordered by the attending physician or surgeon for strictly medicinal use) are charged extra."

The costs are significant to understand some important changes in the Hospital's operations and its basic philosophy. A comparison of salaries in this era is instructive: on average, medical health workers earned $256 per year, public school teachers lived on $328 per year and the average income in all industries was $438 per year. When considering the range of charges for "private" patients, it is obvious that the Jewish Hospital had progressed well beyond merely caring for the indigent; while the Hospital continued in its committment to care for all regardless of ability to pay, a class system also existed.

As was mentioned earlier, even as the new building was dedicated space limitations were becoming apparent. Within two years, surveys of the lots around the existing facility were being conducted as part of long-range planning for expansion. In 1892, the lot adjoining the original building was donated to the association. The cost of $2,600 was covered by $100 donations from twenty-six members of the Cincinnati Jewish community. Still, that left the challenge of construction. Even a promise of a $1,500 gift from Laura Seasongood, a wealthy member of the community, could not cover construction expenses. Given that the debt from the existing building had yet to be paid off, construction on an annex for the Hospital did not begin in earnest until 1897, when bonds were issued to finance the project.

Almost as soon as the annex was finished in the early twentieth century, the association turned its attention to expanding facilities for the nursing school. In September 1902, the board began discussions about the need for a dormitory and classroom building for the nurses. The board's logic is worth quoting:

> All authorities on the subject of the named Nurses agree that when a Nurse is off duty she is benefited in strength and general usefulness by having a home apart from the Institution as well as advantageous to the institution.

Since Joseph Joseph offered to build a nurses' home with a pledge of $15,000, construction began relatively quickly. The addition of the annex and nurses' home was followed in rapid succession by the building of an isolation ward, a surgical center, a children's ward and then the power plant and laundry buildings. The need to build a children's ward was first discussed in 1902 and was justified in part because the existing facility was "too hot in summertime"—perhaps the earliest references to an environmental health concern expressed by the board.

By 1916, the lot at Burnet and Union Street was becoming crowded, at least by the standards of the day, and the Jewish Hospital might more accurately be described as either a campus or medical complex. Whatever the designation, the Hospital served to anchor further development of Cincinnati's medical establishments, for when the city of Cincinnati chose to build its new general hospital complex in 1911, it chose the area adjacent to the Jewish Hospital.

If the Burnet Avenue location was getting crowded with buildings, it was also experiencing a rapid growth in the patient population. According to Hospital records, 2,139 patients passed through the Hospital in 1913,

THE WIFE AND CHILDREN OF

JOSEPH JOSEPH

EMULATING HIS EXAMPLE
AND REVERING HIS MEMORY
HAVE ERECTED AND EQUIPPED

THIS ADDITION TO

THE NURSES HALL

THAT HAD BEEN ERECTED BY HIM
AND MAINTAINED BY THEM

1916

Memorial plaque honoring Cincinnati philanthropist Joseph Joseph's sponsoring of the building of a new nurses' home. In the mid-1930s, his son refused to serve on the board because it tore down the structure to make room for a larger facility. *Photo by author.*

The Jewish Hospital complex shortly after the completion of the new nurses' home (on the extreme left of the photograph).

Reading room in the Nurses' Hall of the Jewish Hospital. Nurses, physicians, staff and even patients could sit together.

and this increased to 2,617 in 1914. Since the Hospital was directing those patients who needed long-term care to the "Jewish Convalescent Home," it is likely that most of these patients stayed only brief periods. It is interesting to note that throughout this era the association focused a great deal of effort on building the nursing program and staff. In October 1916, the association president noted, "When the first building of the Hospital was erected, no provision, whatever, was made for nursing, as nursing was then considered unimportant. Now it has become one of the most important branches of our Hospital."

In order to encourage greater professionalization, the nurses' building had a study hall added in 1917, shortly after construction was completed. One final story as to the increased importance of the nursing staff comes from October 1918, during the height of the world influenza pandemic. The Red Cross had contacted the Hospital to inquire about the availability of beds for flu patients; given the virulence of the disease, victims had to be isolated. Although the board initially expressed a willingness to help, the medical staff rejected the request, as the Hospital did not have the capacity to provide the necessary isolation protocols. The overruling of the board by the physicians is indicative of the greater power the professional staff had over the day-to-day operations of the Hospital. While the association was unable to provide bed space, it did, however, promise that should isolation facilities become available at any other hospital, nursing staff from the Jewish Hospital would be provided. No mention was made of physician assistance.

THE BECKMAN DISPENSARY

We need to break our focus away from the Jewish Hospital for a brief time to examine the founding and mission of the Beckman Dispensary, another Cincinnati philanthropic organization dedicated to serving the medical needs of the Jewish community. An examination of the Beckman Dispensary, and how its history intersects with the Jewish Hospital, reveals interesting changes in the wider world of Cincinnati medicine.

Even after the migration of large parts of the Jewish community to Avondale and other suburbs, there remained a substantial number of poor and indigent downtown. These people either could not or would not avail themselves of the services of the Jewish Hospital. It is possible that the distance to the Hospital was too great for some, especially the elderly poor, or it may be a reflection of the Jewish Hospital's creation of the two-tiered system of treating private patients and charity cases differently. For whatever reason, in the early twentieth century it was noted by communal leaders of

The original staff of the Beckman Dispensary in 1910. Boris Bogan, noted social worker, sits in the middle of the group.

Jewish charitable organizations that a large population of the poor lacked access to medical care.

The Cincinnati Jewish community had an active set of social service organizations, which in the early twentieth century were organized into the United Jewish Charities under the leadership of Boris Bogen, a Russian Jewish immigrant and a pioneer in modern social work. In August 1909, the clothing manufacturer N. Henry Beckman gave a bequest in honor of his parents for the establishment of a free dispensary for the poor. The Wilhelm and Bette Beckman Dispensary opened in 1910 at 731 West Sixth Street in downtown Cincinnati, where it was adjacent to the offices of the United Jewish Charities. Bogen and the UJC were tasked with administering the Beckman bequest and supervising the operation of the dispensary.

The initial staff of the Beckman Dispensary apparently worked part time and was made up of Chief Physician Dr. Louis G. Heyn, along with Moses Salazar and Millard Walenstein. An obstetrician, Dr. Ruth Bernheim, was also on staff. In addition to seeing patients at the West Sixth Street location, the Beckman Dispensary staff was mobile, traveling to see patients—what we would call house calls today. According to their records, during the first year of operation they logged more than 3,300 patient visits and 193 house calls.

In 1916, the dispensary hired its first full-time physician, Dr. Hiram B. Weis, a recent graduate of the University of Cincinnati Medical School who had also been one of the first to do residency in the newly completed

Dr. Hiram B. Weis with Dr. Samuel Rabkin and Dr. Sidney J. Rauh; they were the first full-time physicians and dentists working for the Beckman Dispensary.

Cincinnati General Hospital. Weis was also affiliated with the Jewish Hospital. Weis not only saw patients but also helped expand the scope of the dispensary. Two dentists, Dr. Samuel Rabkin and Dr. Sidney J. Rauh, were also brought on to the staff.

Staff of the Beckman Dispensary, circa 1916. Dr. Hiram Weis is in the center.

In 1918, the Beckman Dispensary was put under the aegis of the Jewish Hospital, although it retained its separate identify and funding. This administrative move is interesting in that it enabled the dispensary to expand its access to the medical specialists of the Jewish Hospital, including having the services of the Hospital nurses, but it raises an interesting question: what benefit accrued to the Hospital?

One possible explanation lies in understanding the target audience of the Beckman Dispensary, which was discussed at a May 1921 meeting of the Dispensary Board. The meeting generated a profile of the three distinct populations served by dispensary: first was what was termed a "relief" group of families who came to the dispensary and could not pay at all for services. This made up about 50 percent of all patients. The second population was a "borderline" group, composing about 48 percent of families seen by dispensary staff and in which paying for services was a hardship. The third group, made up of 2 percent of the families, could pay for all services.

It seems likely that in this period, immediately following the ending of World War I and the influenza pandemic, the Jewish Hospital was struggling to maintain its commitment to care of the indigent and poor. Indeed, during a medical staff meeting in October 1917, one of the physicians, Dr. Victor Greenbaum, claimed that Cincinnati General Hospital was treating a greater number of the Jewish poor than the Jewish Hospital. Greenbaum even suggested that this might be a conscious policy of some members of the Hospital's administration. Despite such accusations, we can find proof that the association was still committed to serving the poor in a variety of documents. For example, the annual report for 1920 described the establishment of an "eye clinic for the benefit of the poor." As the report highlighted the work of the clinic in saving the eyesight of an elderly patient resident in the Old Aged Home, as well as restoring the sight of two children, it obviously sought to emphasize the Hospital's continued commitment to philanthropic activities, even if in a somewhat defensive tone. Despite highlighting such activities in its reports to the community, however, the association was undergoing some fundamental changes.

Before the Progressive Era, philanthropic groups, such as the board of the Jewish Hospital, regarded themselves as the guardians of the poor. By 1920, the association was starting to regard itself more as financial manager of a nonprofit organization. While the Hospital was still open to all, regardless of the ability to pay, the costs of management and services, simply put, had made it difficult to take in as many charity cases as in the past. Therefore, the board was looking for various mechanisms to either save money or utilize resources more effectively. One example of economizing involved what might be likened to a pharmaceutical cooperative. In 1921, the Jewish Hospital joined the Cincinnati Economy Drug Company, for a membership fee of $25. The association then deposited another $100 in order to purchase drugs when the Hospital required them. The existence of such organizations, which likely served a variety of hospitals and physicians in the city, is one example of the application of modern business methods to medical care—in this case on the pharmaceutical side.

If we keep in mind the financial issues, then incorporating the Beckman Dispensary more closely into the Hospital's orbit makes a great deal of sense. The dispensary's mission was similar to the Hospital's—service to the poor and indigent—and the addition of the dispensary enabled the association to retain one of its core missions without having to heavily subsidize it. The challenge facing both institutions was one of apportionment of resources, both staff and financial.

By January 1922, the relationship between the Jewish Hospital and the Beckman Dispensary was achieving a higher level of coordination. A joint

Certificate of membership in the Cincinnati Economy Drug Club. Such organizations ensured that the Jewish Hospital was able to obtain pharmaceuticals at affordable prices.

committee of the United Jewish Charities and Hospital Association arrived at a working plan. The Beckman Dispensary, under a director jointly appointed by the Hospital and Social Services Agency, would take over a portion the outpatient work of the Jewish Hospital specifically relating to general medical care, dental treatment and pediatrics. As soon as the Hospital was ready, it would take over from the dispensary the care of gynecological cases and run a skin clinic. In addition, the Hospital would be responsible for cardiovascular as well as ear, nose and throat treatment. While the Hospital and the Beckman Dispensary committed themselves to "the closest cooperation," financial issues were not discussed in the planning meeting.

In addition to taking on many of the charity cases for the Hospital, the Beckman Dispensary treated its clients on an outpatient basis, meaning that less hospital space was needed for it to function. Furthermore, since the dispensary made house calls, not all of its patients came to the Hospital on Burnet Avenue. This likely provided an additional windfall for an institution that was starting to struggle with a shortage of beds and was trying to expand its patient capacity.

One clue as to the funding sources comes from the association's annual reports. In the 1919 annual report from the board's financial secretary, no mention was made as to the cost to the Hospital of charity cases.

Although they were likely covered under "General Expense," the report did list how much money was brought in from serving private patients. In addition to private donations, bequests and money from the United Jewish Charity, in 1920 the board also began to draw money from Cincinnati's Community Chest to help fund the Hospital. During the Progressive Era, the centralization and rationalization of charity distribution led many cities to create Community Chest organizations, which were funds for

CINCINNATI COMMUNITY CHEST

EXECUTIVE DEPARTMENT

CINCINNATI, OHIO

December 6, 1920

Jewish Hospital Association
Burnet Ave. & Union
Cincinnati, Ohio

Gentlemen:

      Mr. Maurice J. Freiberg brought to my attention your plans for raising money for capital investment purposes, money, as I understand it, which will be needed for buildings, grounds, repairs and for deficits which have been occasioned very largely through building operation.

      May I assure you and through you anyone who may inquire, that no part of this expenditure is taken care of by the Community Chest and that your raising of funds for this purpose in no way conflicts with the policies of the Community Chest.

      We are contributing to your current expense charity deficit, and have nothing whatsoever to do with your capital investment.

Very truly yours,

C M Bookman

Letter from the Cincinnati Community Chest. By 1920, the Jewish Hospital was treating a number of non-Jewish charity patients and was able to drawn on money from beyond the Jewish community.

welfare activities supported by voluntary contributions, and yet distribution to private welfare organizations was often determined by civic officials. Access to Community Chest money probably helped fund the work of the Beckman Dispensary, as well as the charity cases treated by the Hospital. A February 1922 financial report to the board broke down the percentages:

30% full pay
30% part pay (3.00 per day)
40% free

The report did not break down what percentage of the free patients were treated by the Beckman Dispensary. Appeals to the Community Chest for funds indicate how thoroughly the Hospital was integrated into the philanthropic network of the city through its charitable work. A December 1920 letter from the Community Chest also indicates that the money was not to be used toward the ongoing capital fundraising and physical expansion of the Hospital.

The Jewish Hospital After 1920

By 1920, the original Burnet Avenue building was being utilized as a patient ward, while the annex had become the main hospital building, with the operating center attached. The expanded Nurses' Hall sat on the extreme left of the complex and had classroom space in addition to serving as a dormitory. In order to more efficiently run the school and manage the nursing staff, the job of the superintendent of nurses was separated from that of head of the nursing school, another example of progressive management at work.

The Jewish Hospital also began to further expand its services into a new area. While the Hospital had obstetricians and gynecologists on staff since the late nineteenth century, and childbearing services were obviously available to patients, by 1920 one of the growth areas for private patients was in maternity services. As such, the Hospital began its latest initiative: to create a dedicated maternity ward.

It is important to keep in mind that while Progressive Era physicians were expected to be more highly trained and Hospital administration were developing concepts of scientific management, city and state governments were also expanding their supervision of public health institutions. In the

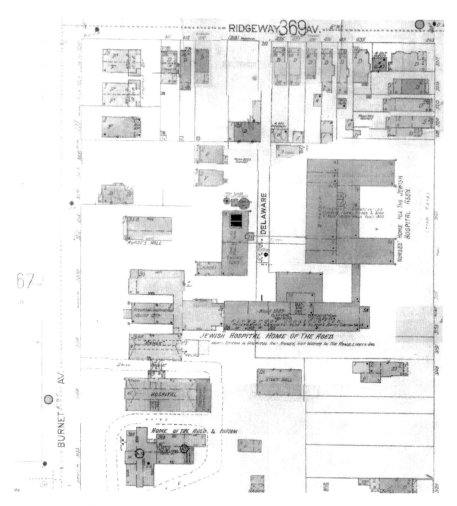

The Sanborn maps were originally created to estimate fire insurance rates. This map, originally produced in the early twentieth century, contains handwritten notes of the Pill Hill area circa 1922. *Courtesy Cincinnati Public Library.*

early twentieth century, the State of Ohio and the City of Cincinnati had reputations for progressive boards of health and were committed to greater supervision of hospitals. As such, while the association was engaged in a fundraising campaign to build a maternity wing, the Hospital administrators worked with the medical staff to gain the state certification that would qualify them to serve as a maternity hospital.

The building of a maternity wing and the requisite state certification vividly illustrate the evolution of the Jewish Hospital during the

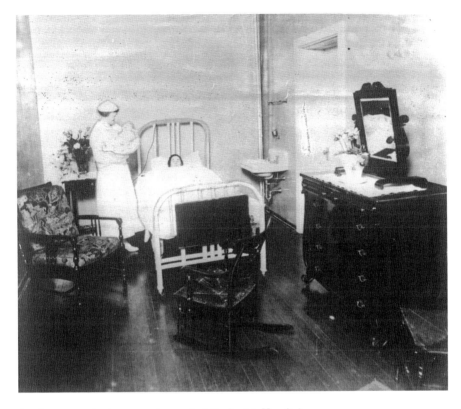

A private room in the maternity ward of the Jewish Hospital.

Progressive Era. The planning for Hospital renovation was entrusted to an architectural group called Berlin, Schwerin and Kendall, which was charged with crafting "a plan for the further development of the Hospital including the Martha Pritz Freiberg Maternity Pavilion." The plans included a systematic layout of a general maternity ward, which was not private, along with private rooms priced at five dollars per day. In addition, the inclusion of a nursery, baths and a porch to ensure that patients had access to fresh air demonstrated a trend toward environmental health. As part of the proposed expansion, the Hospital also renovated its main entryway, which remained in place until the massive renovation project in the 1960s changed the very shape of the entire complex.

As the maternity wing was being constructed, the association received its permit from the State Department of Health—License No. 256—which granted the Hospital the right to "conduct and maintain a Maternity Hospital, Maternity Home or Lying-in Hospital." While the Hospital was

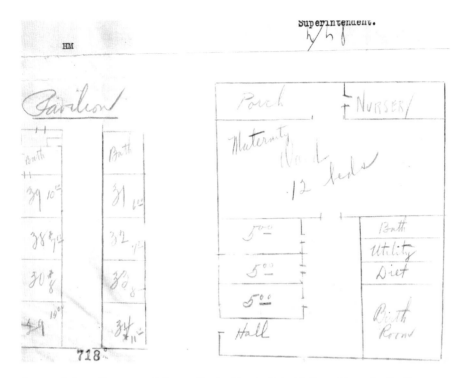

Proposed chart of rooms and charges for the Martha Pritz Freiberg Maternity Pavilion. Note the various room sizes and emphasis on access to fresh air.

limited to no more than fifteen patients and fifteen infants, it nonetheless marked a further expansion of services available to the community.

The October 1922 dedication ceremony celebrated more than the building of the Maternity Pavilion and a new front entrance. Although it was discussed at the beginning of the chapter, it is worth revisiting the dedication for what it can tell us about what did *not* change about the Hospital in more than thirty years. The inclusion of Dr. David Philipson in the ceremony tied the event to the Hospital's history, in part because he was at the 1890 event but also because he was a prominent figure in the Cincinnati Reform Jewish community. Philipson was a protégé of Isaac Mayer Wise and was part of the first class to graduate from Hebrew Union College in 1883. Another tie to tradition was the presence of Dr. Julian Morgenstern, the president of the Hebrew Union College, on the podium to give the benediction, much as Isaac Mayer Wise had done in 1890. Oddly enough, Morgenstern was not listed on the program and was apparently a last-minute addition. The presence of Philipson and Morgenstern reminded the audience of the Hospital's history and also the connection between two of

STATE DEPARTMENT OF HEALTH

License to Conduct Maternity Hospital, **Maternity Home or Lying-in Hospital**

License No. 256

TO WHOM IT MAY CONCERN:

This is to Certify that, in accordance with the provisions of Section 6259 of the General Code of Ohio, the State Department of Health, by its duly authorized representative, has made an investigation of .... The Jewish Hospital .... located at .... Burnet Ave., Cincinnati ...., Ohio.

The State Department of Health hereby grants this license to conduct and maintain a Maternity Hospital, Maternity Home or Lying-in Hospital.

The number of women permitted to be received and kept at any one time for the purpose of confinement in the premises, above described, shall not exceed 15, the number of infants shall not exceed 15

This license shall continue in full force and effect for one year from .... January 1 ...., 19 21., unless sooner revoked for cause.

Issued to

........Samuel Straus........

....................President,..........

Witness my hand and the seal of the State Department of Health this ...9....day of.........February...., A. D. 19 21.

Commissioner of Health.

250—7-19—767

License from the State of Ohio giving the Jewish Hospital the authority to operate as a maternity hospital.

the iconic institutions of Cincinnati Jewish life, for while the Hospital was not an arm of the Reform movement, many of its founders and current leaders were members of Reform congregations. Thus while eastern European immigration changed the demographic profile of Cincinnati Jewry, the board was still dominated by the old guard of German Jewish families.

As we have seen, the original hospital building on Burnet Avenue was the result of fundamental shifts in both Cincinnati Jewish life and changes in medicine in the wider community. Progressive reformers were not romantics; as the historian David Stradling pointed out, progressive reformers did not yearn for an imagined agrarian past but rather sought to make urban life better by focusing on the development of city infrastructure to promote environmental health. Since its dedication in 1890, the Jewish Hospital Association had not stopped building, following the basic guideline that it could improve the health of its patients, whether they be charity or private, by providing a physical location for healing. The creation of an extensive medical complex, and the expansion of the types of medicine practiced, situated the Jewish Hospital in the forefront of medical practices in the city during the twentieth century.

Medical Portraits at the Turn of the Century

Joseph Ransohoff (1853–1921) is primarily remembered as a professor of Surgery at the University of Cincinnati, where he taught for more than thirty years. He also served as chief of the medical staff at the Jewish Hospital when it moved to Pill Hill, and as such, he played a prominent role in guiding the Hospital as it expanded the size and diversity of its medical staff. Ransohoff's reputation was an important factor in attracting a cadre of qualified physicians to work with him, and this ensured that the Jewish Hospital was in the forefront of progressive medical advances.

Sigmar Stark (1862–1925) was born in the German lands and immigrated to Cincinnati with his parents (his father was also a physician) when he was four. Stark studied medicine at the Bellevue Medical College in New York. After finishing medical school in the United States, a number of Cincinnati's Jewish physicians spent all, or part, of their internships in Europe, particularly at German hospitals. In the late nineteenth and

Graduates of the University of Cincinnati Medical School in the early twentieth century. By the early twentieth century, a symbiotic relationship existed between the Jewish Hospital and UC Medical School.

early twentieth centuries, German medical education and hospitals were considered among the best in the world, and since many of Cincinnati's earliest Jewish physicians were of German extraction, it was a logical connection to return to the old country to complete their education. When Stark returned to Cincinnati, he opened a private practice and was also appointed a gynecologist at the Jewish Hospital, where he remained on staff for much of his career. He also served as a professor of gynecology at the University of Cincinnati, helping to further the close relationship between the Jewish Hospital and the university medical school.

Alfred Friedlander (1871–1939) was born in Cincinnati and obtained his medical degree from the University of Cincinnati; as was common at the time, he spent more than a year in Europe continuing his medical studies. Friedlander was appointed the first pediatrician of the Jewish Hospital on February 5, 1899, and as we saw earlier in this chapter, he played a prominent role in improving the environmental conditions of the pediatric wing of the Hospital. Friedlander's career is indicative of the cross-fertilization that existed between the Jewish Hospital and the University of Cincinnati. A graduate of the latter, he served on the staff of the Hospital after returning to Cincinnati. In addition to teaching at the University of Cincinnati, Friedlander was chief of staff of the Cincinnati General Hospital from 1937 to 1940; at the same time, he served as dean of the UC College of Medicine from 1934 to 1940. At a time when many medical schools in the United States were limiting the number of Jewish students admitted, the University of Cincinnati had a Jewish dean.

Chapter 3

A PROGRESSIVE HOSPITAL IN PEACE, DEPRESSION AND WAR, 1920–1945

April 1922 was supposed to be a joyous time in Point Pleasant, Ohio. As part of the celebration of the centennial birthday of its most famous son, President Ulysses S. Grant, the riverboat *Island Queen* was taking passengers on excursions. On April 27, disaster struck as the hurricane deck on the riverboat collapsed, killing several and injuring many of the passengers. In the chaos that followed, a number of spectators on shore were also hurt, primarily by speeding automobiles.

When word of the disaster reached Cincinnati some twenty-five miles downriver, the Jewish Hospital dispatched an emergency team of half a dozen nurses, two doctors and three ambulances to Point Pleasant, where they established a field hospital to treat the wounded. All told, the emergency team provided medical care to more than two dozen people, among them an eighty-six-year-old veteran of the Grand Army of the Republic who was attending the festivities to honor his old commander, a three-year-old girl who suffered facial lacerations from flying glass and W.T. Warner, the Clermont County coroner, who was injured when a passing automobile struck him as he approached the scene. In fact, Warner suffered a severe fracture to his leg and was subsequently admitted to the Jewish Hospital for treatment. On May 8, 1922, a representative of the U.S. Grant Memorial Centenary wrote to express the "deep appreciation we feel for the important assistance rendered by the Jewish Hospital" and, in particular, complimented the Hospital on the efficiency and organization of the medical team.

The doctors and nurses of the emergency team sent by the Jewish Hospital to help treat victims of the *Island Queen* disaster in April 1922.

While the Point Pleasant incident was a relatively minor affair except for those involved, and though the response of the Jewish Hospital was hardly a mass mobilization of resources, it is nonetheless an instructive example of the state of the institution in 1922. The Hospital learned of the disaster within a short time thanks to the establishment of a modern communication system that had been installed at the facility in the early twentieth century and enabled it to link to city, county and state officials; the Hospital was able to send assistance because it had a fleet of ambulances available to transport medical personal to the scene and the wounded back to the Hospital; and finally, four of the nurses dispatched were, in fact, trainees, an intentional decision on the part of the Hospital Administration—in addition to the incident being a teachable moment, the organization knew from a master schedule how many and which trainees were available. Simply put, the Jewish Hospital had planned ahead to respond to such emergencies, an example of Progressive management ideas put into practice.

It is a historical truism that after 1918 the United States had tired of Progressive reforms and overseas crusades. During the 1920s, as the conventional wisdom goes, American public opinion was marked by a more laissez-faire attitude toward business regulation, as well as a desire for a government less intrusive in public affairs. Certainly there is a great deal of

The Jewish Hospital Complex in the early twentieth century. The Hospital Association embraced progressive ideas of management. *Courtesy Cincinnati Historical Society.*

truth in this depiction, as American society in the 1920s was characterized by some as the Jazz Age rather than an age of reform. Yet while the Progressive Era might have been over by 1922, its legacy remained in the lasting impact that its ideas about management and organization had on institutions such as the Cincinnati Jewish Hospital.

Like the rest of the United States, Cincinnati in the interwar years was marked by a boom period during the 1920s followed by the bust of the Great Depression, which lasted throughout the 1930s; each decade brought new opportunities and challenges for the Hospital. While the era of mass migration from eastern Europe was over, its impact on the size and diversity of Cincinnati Jewry was now a permanent feature of the communal landscape. Although the old-line German Jewish families continued to dominate the running of many of Cincinnati's Jewish institutions, like the Hospital, communal leaders found themselves struggling to adapt to a population whose religious observance was often more traditional than their own. When it came to Hospital operations, many patients expected such things as kosher food and a place to pray while being treated. Indeed, during the 1920s, when the Hospital began planning for another round of expansion, it included plans for the building of a kosher kitchen. While the advent of the Great Depression forced the Hospital to postpone a number

The Jewish Hospital after the 1922 expansion. The new entranceway is visible in the center of the photograph.

of these plans, it found that some in the community still wanted their ritual needs observed. While financial stability returned to the Hospital in the period leading up to and during World War II, times were still hard. Caring for patients during the war was a challenge, as many doctors, nurses and staff members were called to military service, while wartime shortages of supplies meant that resources were often stretched to the limit.

Yet it was during this tumultuous era of boom, bust and war that the Jewish Hospital established one of the earliest children's mental health clinics in the country, as well as a medical research facility that would soon mark the institution as one of the preeminent research, teaching and treatment centers in the region. As the reputation of Cincinnati's Jewish Hospital grew, medical school graduates from all over the Midwest came to serve their residency in the Queen City.

The Management of the Jewish Hospital

In early April 1920, Lewis Levy, the new superintendent of the Jewish Hospital, issued a report that outlined new procedures that he believed needed to be implemented to improve institutional effectiveness. Levy, a former journalist, had served as superintendent of the Mount Zion Hospital in San Francisco and so came to Cincinnati with a great deal of experience in the application of modern managerial theory. In his report, Levy admitted that while the board cautioned him to "go slowly" in implementing changes, he sometimes approached things with a "western speed," a reference perhaps to being impatient with what he perceived to be the hidebound processes of his new employers.

One of Levy's first suggestions was that the Hospital create two separate sets of patient wards: one set would be for "private and part pay" patients, while the other would be a charity ward. After all, private patients had access to more services than charity patients. The first ward would be

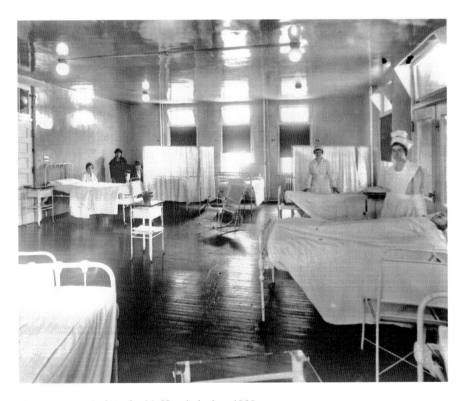

Treatment ward of the Jewish Hospital, circa 1920.

75

reserved for those who could pay all or at least part of the costs of their care. As for the other group, Levy recommended that only those patients sent by the United Jewish Charities or admitted by physicians should be admitted directly to the charity wards. Every morning, the United Jewish Charity's representative at the Hospital—today we would call them social workers or patient advocates—would be tasked with "investigating" new patients and confirming to the superintendent that they were, in fact, genuine charity cases. This recommendation implies that up to that point private and charity patients were mixed together, and this may have been a cause of social tension.

While a more rigid segregation of private and charity patients at the Hospital may look to modern eyes like a class-based version of Jim Crow, Levy did set the bar of qualifying for the first ward at the low level of one dollar per day. Levy argued that the Hospital needed this new system in order to achieve a more rational accounting procedure, whereby funds from paying patients could be channeled to Hospital operations. Levy also argued that by segregating patients in this way the Hospital would develop a better sense of its income stream. With a more accurate accounting of income, it would then be possible to assess how much money needed to be raised to support charity cases. In addition, Levy's plans called for updating daily rates for private patients in order to bring those in line with actual costs.

Levy also focused on several processes for environmental health. He remarked on the salutary effect of regularly washing down the walls and floor of the surgery and how the installation of new fans in the surgical center would help reduce summer heat. He also consulted with the medical staff to develop recommendations for a new set of rates for surgical services.

While Levy's report covered such mundane matters as efficiencies in purchasing supplies and how best to handle billing for such things as laboratory services, it also revealed the financial and administrative consequences of some of the relatively new developments in medical science. For example, Levy reported, "The xray [sic] department will soon be in order. Plates will be properly filed away and it will be conducted along business lines." The development of X-ray technology, first introduced at the Jewish Hospital in the prewar years, was made possible by the donation of equipment, while the funds to maintain this new technology and utilize it had to come from the regular Hospital budget. It also created a new challenge: what to do with the X-rays themselves. In another example of Progressive management practices, Levy arranged for the construction of a specially built vault to house patient X-rays in environmentally safe conditions.

One of Superintendent Levy's projects was the creation of a vault to house patient X-rays in environmentally controlled conditions. *Courtesy Cincinnati Historical Society.*

Some of Levy's reforms might seem obvious to the modern eye. For example, he advocated posting pharmacy hours on the door for the benefit of the patients, the hiring of additional kitchen staff to maintain services during peak hours and the installation of larger "ice-boxes" (refrigerators) to preserve food. Yet the fact that he included such information in his report indicates that prior to his arrival such practices were not part of the Hospital's regular protocols.

Levy's suggestions for administrative change did not come cheap, and in a follow-up report, the superintendent argued that the Hospital needed to add six new staff personnel: one assistant bookkeeper and cashier to expedite financial matters, especially routine bills; one information and room clerk who would greet people as they entered the Hospital and direct them to their destination; one "Elevator Man" who would be on duty from 8:00 a.m. to 5:30 p.m. and whose presence would add to the safety of its operation (presumably the elevator operator would also be capable of providing routine maintenance); one window washer and "all around man" who could also serve as a messenger; and two "colored" maids who would be paid $1.64 per week—not surprisingly, the lowest rate of any of the new staffers. All

The pharmacy of the Jewish Hospital, circa 1920. One of Superintendent Levy's reforms was to put its operating hours on the door.

told, Levy calculated that his reforms would require $1,090.00 in additional payroll, an increase of almost 30 percent from the existing payroll of $3,875.00. Incidentally, this increase did not include his superintendent's salary of $625.00 per month. Levy's reforms were apparently not too controversial for the board, as they were largely implemented. Levy was also one of the first to argue that it was necessary to "liven up" the front entrance, something that was part of the renovations finished in 1922, as discussed in the last chapter.

Over the next few months, Levy engaged in a number of modifications to Hospital procedures and also served in an advisory capacity in developing the plans for the new maternity wing. Levy was also authorized to contact other Jewish Hospital in the United States in order to get comparison information on new types of equipment, ranging from oxygen machines for the surgery to Singer sewing machines for the laundry. He was also asked to communicate with "the various Jewish Hospitals of this country with a view to learning whether the installation of a kosher kitchen was feasible and a success." More than seventy years after the Jewish Hospital's founding, this seems to have been the first official discussion of whether a kosher kitchen was practical.

The timing of this discussion about installing a kosher kitchen certainly reflects the changing dynamic within the Cincinnati Jewish community. As we shall see, it took nearly two more decades to bring kosher food to the Hospital, and its implementation caused a certain amount of controversy.

Levy represented a new type of administrator for the Jewish Hospital, a technocrat whose goal was to achieve the highest level of efficiency for his institution. As a former journalist, Levy also understood that he was the logical person to raise the profile of the Jewish Hospital in various national periodicals. For example, in an article published in the May 1925 issue of the journal *Modern Hospital*, Levy recounted the process of the 1922 renovation and expansion, with an emphasis on the physical infrastructure and ease of cleaning that not only defined a modern hospital building's appearance but also promoted the health of patients. In "80 Trays Served in 30 Minutes on Any Day of the Week," an article for *Hospital Management* (January 1927), Levy explained how the Jewish Hospital was able to produce eighty trays of food for patients in a mere thirty minutes. As befits a technical publication, the article is painstaking in its description of the process, from the generating of the menu to the delivery of the food, yet it is also interesting for two related reasons: Levy described the work of the three professional dietitians employed by the Hospital—another one of his reforms—and there is no mention of kosher food.

Indeed, most of Levy's published work, as well as his reports to the board, are devoid of any religious references or even the philosophical underpinnings that can be found in similar material generated by the lay leaders of the association. It is not that Levy lacked philanthropic commitment or even a Jewish identity; rather, he has to be understood as that breed of administrator whose job it was to implement the philosophical goals of his employer, in this case the board of trustees of the Jewish Hospital. As a modern manager, his decisions were largely controlled by his sense of what could be accomplished given the physical layout of his institution and the budget he managed. Yet it would not be fair to say that Levy did not understand the mission of the Hospital, especially when it came to charity cases. Levy asserted in one of his earliest reports that charity patients were deserving of respect and kindness. At one point, he wrote, "My plans call for a better treatment of our free patients, which I am sure is what you gentleman require and expect. This

80 Trays Served in 30 Minutes on "Any Day in the Week"

BY LOUIS COOPER LEVY,
Superintendent, Jewish Hospital, Cincinnati, O.

EIGHTY trays, complete in every particular, delivered to private patients in thirty minutes!

Such is the boast of the Jewish Hospital of Cincinnati. The reader of this article immediately raises a doubt in his or her mind, and undoubtedly declares "It can't be done!"

Doubters are invited to a demonstration any day in the week and at any time.

I recall at an Ohio state convention a number of dietitians and architects present expressed the same doubt and accepted an invitation to see the "phenomenon" with their own eyes. This they did and the "doubting Thomases" or "Thomasees" went away fully convinced.

How It Is Accomplished

System and the expenditure of money will solve any difficulty that you may have in handling tray service. Our method is so simple that I marvel at the expense and antiquated way some institutions handle private patients' trays.

I have studied the situation in many hospitals and find that trays are handled in the following manner:

A. The food is sent upstairs in containers and the food ladled out on the trays, and then carried by nurses to the patient. This means congestion in the small diet kitchens, extra maid service and the presence of a dietitian.

B. Semi-completed trays are placed on the food cart and when six or more are completed the cart is pushed on the elevator and taken to the floor diet kitchen. Then the special nurses and pupil nurses elbow each other, striving to get coffee, toast, bread, etc., for their particular tray. After all this is done, the food getting cold in the meantime, the tray is carried to the patient.

C. Actual cooking on the floor, filling the corridors with odors, the trays being set up in the diet kitchen and then carried to the patient. This necessitates extra maid service, the presence of a dietitian to supervise the trays and the carrying

LOUIS C. LEVY

Mr. Levy began his business career as a newspaper man and was Washington and New York correspondent for the San Francisco Examiner. About thirteen years ago he became affiliated with the Mt. Zion Hospital, San Francisco, and made such a splendid record that the Jewish Hospital of Cincinnati called him and he has been in charge of that institution for the past seven years. He has contributed a number of articles on hospital administration to HOSPITAL MANAGEMENT and other journals, and also has taken an active part in discussions at various conventions.

of trays down long corridors to the patients.

D. The completing of individual trays, carrying them to the dumb waiter, sending them to the floor, taking off the tray and again carrying it to the patient. This means delay and extra help also.

A Simplified Method

How much simpler is the system in vogue at the Jewish Hospital!

I am not exaggerating when I declare that eighty completed trays reach the patients in thirty minutes. This statement is explained in this article, but I extend a cordial invitation to executives and dietitians to visit our institution to prove or disprove my assertion.

All this is accomplished in a simple manner.

At the outset let me state we have three dietitians, Miss Velma Nelp, graduate of Ohio State University; Miss Agnes Cantrell, graduate of State Normal School,

Athens, Ga., and Miss Marian Risburg, graduate of Lombard College Galesburg, Ill. They are enthusiastic in their commendation of the system. Their views are worth while because of their experience and knowledge of methods in vogue in other hospitals.

Each morning the floor nurse visits the patient to learn the selection for the morrow's meals. The patient's wishes are in conformity with the diet specified by the attending physician.

After viewing the menu, the patient tells what she desires and this is noted on a blank—what kind of eggs, cereal, bread or toast, fruit and beverage he is to have for breakfast; or what kind of soup, meat, potatoes, vegetables, salad, dessert and beverage for dinner; and the kind of meat, potatoes, vegetables, entree, dessert and beverage for supper.

Carbon copies are made of this order, specifying the number of the room. One copy is kept in the chart room of the floor for checking if necessary, and two copies are collected by the dietitian or assistant at one o'clock each day.

The dietitian takes off of these sheets the number of soups, meats, etc., so that the cooks know how much to prepare and have ready for the following day's meals.

Another copy is cut up in squares and each square is placed on the tray for future checking.

For illustration:

BREAKFAST

Eggs, poached
Cereal, oatmeal
Bread, yes
Fruit, oranges
Beverage, cocoa
Room 101

DINNER

Soup, Julienne
Meat, chicken a la Maryland
Potatoes, Duchess
Vegetables, green bean succotash
Salad, head lettuce, French dressing
Dessert, snow flurry
Beverage, tea
Room 101

SUPPER

Soup, consomme
Meat, cold cuts

Title page of Louis Levy's article for the journal *Hotel Management*. As a former journalist, Levy understood the importance of publicizing the work of the Jewish Hospital.

The kitchen of the Jewish Hospital after its expansion in 1922. It was not yet able to provide kosher food. *Courtesy Cincinnati Historical Society.*

will be done by giving them hotter and better food, a tray cloth on their tray and a napkin. Their comfort and care is my earnest desire and I am sure you will hear good reports in the future." Some would suggest that Levy's association of kindness and respect with hot food is a very Jewish trait.

By the time of Levy's appointment in 1920, the essential relationship of the board to the day-to-day running of the Hospital was much different than it had been when the *Rules and Regulations* of the Hospital had been published twenty-two years earlier. The board no longer appointed a Visitors Committee every month to check on the patients and ensure that the staff was compliant with the rules. Now a cadre of professional administrators generated reports on everything from the number of patients treated to the average length of hospitalization, what these patients were treated for and how many patients had died while in Hospital care.

Even the relationship between the medical staff and the board had evolved dramatically since 1898. For example, in the late nineteenth century the board appointed the medical staff directly, while in 1920 it was the medical staff

Dr. Hiram Weis consulting with a patient. By 1920, the medical staff was no longer appointed directly by the association board; rather, staff were nominated by fellow physicians.

itself that recommended physicians for staff appointments. While the board would then vote to approve or reject the selection, it is significant that the board rarely voted down a nomination from the medical staff. In June 1922, for example, the medical staff submitted an organizational chart to the board for its approval. The chart divided the physicians into seventeen specialties, each with a director, an attending physician, an assistant attending physician and a consultant (although only a few areas listed such a person). The different fields of medicine were as follows:

- *Surgery*
- *Proctology*
- *Orthopedics*
- *Internal Medicine*
- *Gynecology*
- *Genito-Urinary* [in modern parlance genitourinary system]
- *Neurology*

The library of the Jewish Hospital in the early 1920s. A pleasant environment was considered an essential part of Hospital life.

- *Opthalmology*
- *Oto-Laryngology* [ear, nose and throat]
- *Pediatrics*
- *Obstetrics*
- *Dermatology*
- *Anesthesia*
- *Dentistry*
- *Roengenology* [roentgenology or radiation/X-ray; apparently spelled wrong in the document]
- *Pathology*
- *Department of Psychopathic Institute*

This organizational chart is instructive, as many of the specialties found at the Jewish Hospital in 1922 are still recognizable today. Meanwhile, the organization of doctors into the categories of director, attending physician, assistant and consultant was one that most hospitals adopted during this era. Of particular interest was the last specialty, Department of Psychopathic Institute, held by Dr. Louis A. Lurie. This institute was one of the cutting-edge medical advances of the Jewish Hospital in the twentieth century, and it is to its story that we now turn.

THE CHILDREN'S PSYCHOPATHIC INSTITUTE

In the summer of 1920, the "Red House," a disused dwelling on Harvey Avenue adjacent to the main Hospital complex, was repainted and rewired at a cost of just over $800 in order to prepare the house to serve as the headquarters for an experiment. While the Red House was considered inadequate to house employees of the Hospital, it was considered "ideal for the Psychopathic experiment"—or, more precisely, as the home for the newly established Children's Psychopathic Institute, one of the first such establishments in the country for treating mental illness in children.

The Jewish Hospital was no stranger to pediatric care. The existence of a specialized children's ward at the Jewish Hospital dates from the early twentieth century, when it was situated on the third floor of the main building. Throughout the early part of the twentieth century, a variety of Hospital physicians sought to improve pediatric care. For example, on March 3, 1901, Dr. Alfred Friedlander, one of the Hospital's physicians, argued that the current accommodations were an unhealthy environment in which to treat children. Friedlander argued that in summer, the lack of ventilation made the rooms "almost stifling," and in addition, the ward lacked access

View of the Jewish Hospital in 1922, the first home of the Psychopathic Institute (on the left).

to sunlight and fresh air, which he argued were "indispensable if we are to secure good results" for pediatric patients. Recognizing that creating new space for the children was a financial challenge for the Hospital, Friedlander offered to help raise funds for building a summer pavilion. He was, in fact, able to raise $27,500, and the pavilion was completed in 1904.

Friedlander's efforts on behalf of expanding the Hospital's treatment of pediatric patients were aided by the development of a nascent program in mental hygiene at the neighboring University of Cincinnati Medical School. Just as modern methods of social services were developing in the early twentieth century, some of which helped create the Beckman Dispensary, so, too, were the fields of psychiatry and psychoanalysis becoming mainstream. In these early days of the field, however, few therapists applied their concepts to children. One group that did advance the notion that mental health issues were important in pediatric care was the United Jewish Social Agencies of Cincinnati.

In 1916, United Jewish Social Agencies was concerned that children were being committed to long-term incarceration as mental patients without the benefit of medical evaluation and care. In order to address these concerns, they created and funded a Committee on Juvenile Research, with a mandate to study "feeblemindedness, delinquency, and kindred conditions." In the early twentieth century, mental health issues were often tied to notions of race, gender and socioeconomic status. After all, until the early twentieth century, "hysteria" was considered a female disorder caused by the irritation of the reproductive organs. Social scientists often linked urban life to various forms of "degeneration," which were often manifested in children's misbehaving. The fact that many of those diagnosed with degenerative disorder came from a lower social order, and did not have access to fresh air and proper hygiene, speaks to the class basis of their assumptions. Terms popular at the time ranged from *idiot* to *cretin*, and the most common way of dealing with such cases was incarceration or at least rigorous supervision. What made the Cincinnati social workers atypical is their insistence that many patients could be treated, if properly diagnosed, and returned to the community.

Given the class dimension in mental health assumptions, it is not surprising that the institution often tasked with treating troubled children was the Beckman Dispensary, whose reports noted a rise in the "large number of nervous, maladjusted, and psychopathic children" who came to the clinic. Many of the children examined were considered mentally deficient, and the social service agency felt that greater time and attention had to be given to diagnosis and then treatment, neither of which the dispensary was equipped to do.

The Committee on Juvenile Research recommended establishing what it called the Psychopathic Institute in order to provide proper diagnoses and find an alternative to long-term institutionalization. While negotiations were opened in 1917 to provide space, administrative supervision and medical services, it was not until 1920 that a formal agreement between the Hospital and the United Jewish Social Agencies was reached. The United Jewish Social Agencies provided $1,000 to finance the institute, and the Hospital loaned it the use of the Red House as a facility for the Psychopathic Institute for Child Care. Dr. Louis A. Lurie, a recent graduate of the University of Cincinnati Medical School, was the founding director. While initially the institute was under the aegis of the United Jewish Social Services, Lurie arranged for the Jewish Hospital to assume full control in April 1921 and, in the process, also shortened the name to the Psychopathic Institute. The social service agencies continued to pay the institute $600 per month in exchange for which eight spots at the Red House were reserved for patients recommended by the agencies.

Children at play in front of the Psychopathic Institute in the 1920s.

One of the rooms in the Psychopathic Institute. The institute emphasized clean conditions and comfortable surroundings.

As with almost every other division within the Hospital, the institute was organized along modern managerial lines. When a child was recommended for admission, he or she was first sent to the Children's Ward of the Hospital for physical evaluation and tests. Some of these tests, such as an X-ray of the skull, reflect the conventional medical wisdom of the times that the size and shape of the head revealed the intellectual and mental capacity of the individual. Once the medical tests were completed, the child was transferred to the Red House, where a professional social worker provided day-to-day supervision and physicians such as Lurie developed a profile of the malady and arranged a course of treatment. The goal of the institute was to try and create an environment designed to help the patients achieve a level of independence and self-sufficiency, thereby enabling them to become productive members of society.

Among the institute's early supporters in the community was Rabbi Michael Aaronsohn. Aaronsohn, who was blinded by an artillery shell during the Battle of the Meuse-Argonne in 1918, graduated from the University of

Rabbi Michael Aaronsohn, a disabled American veteran, sits in the common room of the Psychopathic Institute with some of the patients.

Cincinnati and was ordained at Hebrew Union College in 1923. During his rabbinic career, Aaronsohn promoted a number of causes associated with the mental and physically disabled and even served a term as president of the Hamilton County (Ohio) Council for Retarded Children. His activities on behalf of the institute helped bring it greater acceptance in the community.

Like many of the Hospital's endeavors, the Psychopathic Institute quickly expanded beyond its original facility and found itself short of space and personnel. In the summer of 1929, when the Hospital once again began planning to expand the physical infrastructure of the Hospital complex, it added a commitment to construct a new facility for the Psychopathic Institute to the capital campaign. The timing of this capital campaign was not auspicious, as the stock market crash of late October 1929 ushered in the Great Depression. Not surprisingly, the Hospital's capital campaign stalled. It was, however, an indication of the institute's significance to the community that enough money had been raised to build it a new home by 1932, the only major expansion that the Hospital managed until 1938.

Communal Controversies: Chapel and Kosher Kitchens

As we have seen, the Jewish Hospital first began discussing the issue of installing a kosher kitchen in 1920, when Superintendent Levy was tasked with seeking information from other Jewish hospitals as to the viability of the project. Plans to incorporate a kosher kitchen—which mandated rabbinic supervision and, by implication, required the Hospital to make a foray into communal religious politics—were also part of the 1929 capital campaign. Such an action would bring the Hospital more fully into compliance with traditional Jewish ritual observance, something the association was not always interested in pursuing.

At the same time that plans were underway for a kosher kitchen, other members of Cincinnati's rabbinic establishment wanted the Hospital to

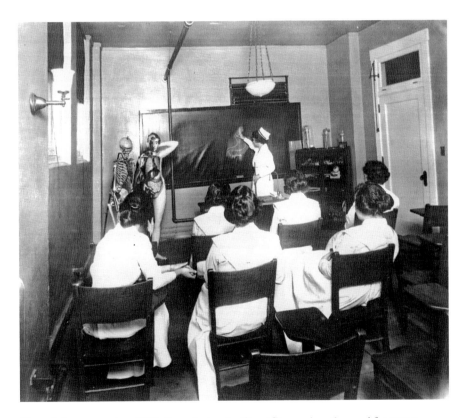

Nurses' classroom, circa 1930. Even during the Great Depression, the need for nurses remained high.

create more Jewish ritual space. On October 17, 1929, Rabbi Samuel Wohl, who was serving as president of the Cincinnati Board of Jewish Ministers (now the Greater Cincinnati Board of Rabbis), wrote to Maurice Pollak, the president of the board, about the need for sacred space at the Hospital. The letter is worth quoting in its entirety:

> *The Rabbis of Cincinnati note with satisfaction the contemplated improvements of the Jewish Hospital.*
>
> *The Jewish community of Cincinnati would be happy to learn that the following recommendations of the Rabbis, unanimously adopted at the meeting of the Board of Jewish Ministers, have received your approval and will be carried out by your Building Committee. We recommend:*
>
> *(a) That a chapel be built to foster the sentiments of worship and meditation in this splendid institution.*
> *(b) In order to meet the religious needs of the Orthodox community, a kosher kitchen is necessary.*
> *(c) In accordance with your promise made last January, the Brit-Milah Room be transferred to a more suitable place.*
>
> *The Board of Jewish Ministers will be happy to transmit to their respective congregations your decision in these matters, and will be happy to co-operate with you for the success of the Jewish Hospital.*

The letter reveals several interesting points about the Hospital's relationship with the local Jewish community. Wohl, who served in the pulpit of K.K. Bene Jeshurun (where Isaac Mayer Wise was rabbi for half a century), was an immigrant from eastern Europe, and while he was ordained by Hebrew Union College as a Reform rabbi, he was more traditional in his practice than the German Jewish elite who ran the Hospital. Incidentally, many of the men who sat on the Hospital's board were members of Wohl's congregation. That Wohl and other rabbis were part of discussions about the building project should not be too surprising, as sustaining the Hospital required communal support, and the rabbis were a logical group to help the board interface with the community.

What is interesting is that the ritual of Brit Milah, the circumcision of Jewish boys, was being carried out at the Jewish Hospital. Official Hospital records, including medical staff reports, contain no reference to the practice being carried out at the institution. How long the Hospital had been hosting the ceremony is not known, although it may have been as recently as 1922, when the opening of the Freiberg Maternity Ward guaranteed that a greater number of children would be born in the Hospital.

In his communication with Maurice Freiberg, who chaired the Building Committee, Pollak indicated that he did not want to commit to any of Rabbi Wohl's recommendations without input from Freiberg's committee. Pollak did, however, acknowledge that some of Wohl's requests were not new: "We have practically conceded that we will take into consideration the installing of a Kosher Kitchen, and we have committed ourselves to take care of Paragraph C namely the Bris-Milah room." Pollak was surprised by the request for a chapel, which he described "as a new one." He concluded that "[w]e have to be very careful and diplomatic in our answer to this Association, in order to hold their good will and have their cooperation and backing from their pulpits."

Freiberg's response to the Wohl letter is also very instructive. After proclaiming that creating a "better Brismilah room in the Hospital" posed no problem, he addressed the issue of the kosher kitchen. Installing a kosher kitchen, according to Freiberg, had received wide discussion, which included soliciting opinions and information from Orthodox groups. He argued that most of those members of the Orthodox community who participated in discussions understood that the board was sympathetic to the idea and that only financial constraints and physical limitations were a hindrance to the "providing of Kosher meals to those orthodox Jews in the hospital, who actually require or desire them."

Freiberg's response to the question of a chapel deserves to be read in full:

> As far as "A" is concerned, that is, the question of building a Chapel in the building, this is a matter that has never had any consideration, and personally, I am not in favor of it. The Jewish Hospital, although its name is Jewish, and the principal support comes from Jews, is a non-sectarian institution. If we had a chapel, I doubt very much whether it would be used much, if at all. It could not be an orthodox chapel; it could not be a Reform Jewish temple, for in that case, no orthodox Jew would use it; and it could scarcely be an open place of Worship, for people of any creed to use, for in that event, my personal opinion is that it would not be used at all.
>
> I fear that there is no place in the hospital for a chapel.

Freiberg's response captured the dilemma facing the Jewish Hospital in this era and even in our own. That the level and style of Jewish religious observance varied between the various streams of Judaism in Cincinnati—Orthodox, Conservative and Reform—has long been understood. But even while a Reform rabbi of Samuel Wohl's stature could express a desire to accommodate traditional dietary rules most often associated with Orthodox Jews, the gap in terms of creating a sacred space in which to pray remained wide. Furthermore, as Freiberg noted, the Jewish Hospital had a long tradition of being nonsectarian, and building any type of chapel, or requiring that all meals served at the Hospital be kosher, risked incurring the wrath of donor groups. Indeed, neither Pollak nor Freiberg advocated turning the Hospital into a totally kosher institution; instead, they only advocated making kosher food available to those who desired to observe the dietary rules.

In his October 30 response to Wohl, Pollak promised that a new space to perform Brit Milah would be provided and also included a resolution passed by the board to assure the community that "as part of the contemplated improvements of the Hospital plant, a Kosher Kitchen be installed." As for the chapel, Pollak told Wohl that "this is an entirely new thought and not being in the present contemplated plan, no definite action was taken, but same will be given future consideration." Wohl was likely experienced enough in communal activities to know that such a response implied it was unlikely to happen. Since no further correspondence on the matter is found in the board records or Wohl's papers, it seems that the issue was quietly dropped.

Black Tuesday occurred the day before Pollak's letter to Wohl, and the collapse of the stock market that began the Great Depression changed the dynamic of the Hospital campaign. Financial constraints meant that with the exception of the Psychopathic Institute, the Jewish Hospital's capital plans were put on hold. While the fundraising continued, it would be nine years before enough money became available for further construction. Meanwhile, the charitable work of the Hospital, including the Beckman Dispensary, was even more in demand as the number of destitute in the city soared. In this context, it is understandable that Maurice Pollak placed the building of a kosher kitchen low on his to-do list. This is why he was probably genuinely surprised at the issue being raised again, rather forcefully, by members of Cincinnati's Orthodox rabbinate in early 1933.

Rabbi Elieazar Silver was the spiritual leader of Kehillah B'nai Israel Congregation in Cincinnati and a member of the Vaad Ho'ier, the Union of Orthodox Jewish Congregations of Greater Cincinnati. On January 11, 1933, he wrote to Maurice Pollak to express his dismay at the failure of the Hospital to build a kosher kitchen. Silver claimed that in

The board of trustees of the Jewish Hospital in 1934, when the issue of building a kosher kitchen was being debated.

previous meetings and communications with the association, he was given assurances that a "plan would be drawn up and that we [the Orthodox congregations] would undertake with funds of our own to build the annex necessary" for a kosher facility. After complaining about the delays, Silver issued a very thinly veiled threat to "bring the matter before the bar of public opinion." Keeping kosher, Silver reminded Pollak, "is a matter of most vital importance to orthodox Jews and therefore we are compelled to press the issue so urgently." Although he ended the letter claiming that he wished to maintain communal harmony, he did not retreat from his demand for prompt action.

The previous four years had not been particularly easy for the Hospital board. In addition to having to put expansion and renovation into abeyance, it often found it difficult to pay its bills. Part of this was obviously the increased strain on Hospital finances from the increased number of charity cases, but the Hospital also had trouble collecting money it was owed. For example, in one case from 1931, a local bank came close to defaulting on paying off assets owed to the Hospital.

In addition to the financial strain, Silver's request also hit a nerve of intra-communal squabbling that existed between the old German Jewish elite, such as Pollak, and more recent immigrants, such as Silver. Despite his position as president of the Jewish Hospital, a communal institution tasked with serving the public, Pollak was also a successful businessman and a respected lay leader. Simply put, he was not necessarily happy when someone made demands on him. Furthermore, while the Orthodox congregations may have pledged money to help build the kosher kitchen, the amount was not sufficient to expand the infrastructure needed to house it, and as such, the installation was still beyond the Hospital's means.

In his January 16 reply to Silver, Pollak denied any recollection of an agreement or understanding on building the kosher kitchen and bluntly told Silver, "I do not like the tone of your letter…which is practically a threat." Pollak asserted, "I tried to make clear to you that under the present conditions and those that have prevailed for the past two or three years, the matter of the completion of our plan has been held up, but by no means abandoned." Indeed, while a survey had been commissioned, which included building a kosher kitchen, Pollak refused to make any promises as to a timeline for construction until existing financial constraints were eased.

The tense communication between the Hospital Board and the Orthodox rabbis led by Silver continued into the summer of 1933, when a petition from the Vaad Ho'ier was submitted on June 15. The petition, which reiterated the demands enunciated by Silver in January, elicited a reply from the association, this time by Maurice Freiberg of the Building Committee. Freiberg informed Rabbi Silver that once the building program was reinitiated, plans for a proper kosher kitchen were included. He ended his letter by stating, "This can only be completed when the available funds are on hand. At the present time, there is no space in the existing Hospital buildings for the placing and establishing of a kosher kitchen."

Silver and the Vaad apparently realized that at the present time they did not have the necessary resources to fund such an endeavor, and furthermore, they did not have many options in the court of public opinion. The Orthodox congregations could boycott the Jewish Hospital if they liked, yet no other public or sectarian medical institution was likely to provide them with access to the necessary dietary requirements. It was not until 1937, when an additional bequest of more than $1,400 was left to the Hospital by one of Rabbi Silver's congregants, did he again raise the issue. In addition to this immediate bequest, Silver also offered to raise another $1,500 from among his congregants. He ended by appealing to the Hospital to give the matter "your kindest attention."

While the tone of this letter was much less threatening than the previous correspondence, its timing was also much more fortuitous, for a year earlier the board had become much more optimistic about its ability to resume construction. While actual work did not begin until early 1938, it did include plans for a kosher kitchen. The kosher kitchen did not, however, become active until April 30, 1939.

Innovations at the Jewish Hospital and the War Years

As we have seen, by the early 1920s the Jewish Hospital had expanded its coverage to include all major fields of medicine. Even in the midst of the Great Depression, it continued to provide care to all, and if the institution was sometimes short of money, it was not only due to the economic downturn. Recognizing that the need for trained nurses remained high, the Hospital utilized much of its endowment to award scholarships for those attending the nursing school, which also helps explain the shortage of funds for capital improvements.

The Hospital was also fortunate that after Louis Levy resigned in February 1930, he was followed by a series of energetic superintendents who managed to keep the Hospital operating, even if they sometimes had to borrow to make payroll. In addition, the Hospital's reputation among medical schools remained high, and its residency program attracted talented physicians from the entire Midwest.

Many of the Hospital's institutions founded in these years would continue to operate well into the postwar era. For example, the Psychopathic Institute, renamed the Child Guidance Home, remained an important part of the Hospital's complex, as did the nursing school, which was moved into a renovated Greenwood Hall, named in honor of the first superintendent of nursing. In 1940, the Beckman Dispensary was moved from its downtown location to the former Nurses' Hall on Burnet Avenue. A primary reason for the move was the conviction of United Jewish Charities that it needed to focus on "education, placement, and economic rehabilitation" and as such turned over operation of the dispensary wholly to the Hospital.

JUNE LEAMAN   LENA M. STOKES   MARGARET ANNA PFLUEGER   AGNES V. MISCHE

The Jewish Hospital

CLASS OF 1938

Jones

\NE M. DUEY   THELMA MARIE KNEPF

Composite photograph of part of the graduating class of the
nurses' school for 1938. During the Great Depression, the Hospital
committed a great deal of money to nursing scholarships.

While some histories of Cincinnati assume this meant the dissolution of
the dispensary, in fact it continued in operation for a number of years. A
better way of describing the change is that it became an outreach arm of
the Hospital Association.

In 1934, the Hospital decided to branch out into an entirely new field:
medical research. Initially, a subcommittee of board members and physicians
was established to study the feasibility of the project, and in 1935, a research
center was formally inaugurated. It was named the May Institute for Medical
Research after a bequest from Mary May, the widow a local physician. The
founding director was Dr. I. Arthur Mirsky, who would run the institute into
the postwar era.

The May Institute's mandate was to provide a linkage between medical
research, medical education and the treatment of patients. The initial focus
of the May Institute was on the study of diabetes, metabolic diseases and
blood clotting, as well as the investigation of the relationship between a
patient's emotional state and their physiological reactions. Initially, the May
Institute was housed in Straus Hall, which had served as one of the classroom
buildings for the nurses' school. It was the intention of the Hospital to build,
once funds became available, a set of purpose-built laboratories for research.

Board of trustees members and professional administrative staff of the Jewish Hospital, circa 1933. The professionalization of management was one of the major innovations of the first part of the twentieth century. *Courtesy Cincinnati Historical Society.*

So, in 1938, when the Hospital felt it could return to its much-delayed building projects, it added a set of plans for a new home for the May Institute. This new optimism was also derailed, but this time not by economic depression, as explained in the annual report for 1941: "Due to the outbreak of the war we had to abandon our plan for building a new laboratory." Mirsky and the May Institute had to settle for rehabilitating existing space.

The end-of-the-year report for 1941, dated December 31, provides a glimpse of how the Jewish Hospital was spending its money. The budget was divided between operating funds and the upkeep of the Hospital Complex, which included the following buildings:

- cottages and bake shop
- power plant and laundry
- Main Building—Hospital Improvement
- Nurses' Hall (New)

- Child Guidance Home
- superintendent's residence
- kosher kitchen
- May Institute for Medical Research building
- May Institute for Medical Research equipment

Total expenditure for the year came to $1,617,257.90, with an unexpended surplus of less than $9,000. Interestingly, the expenditure on the kosher kitchen was listed as $33 in the 1939 report and had increased to $12,333 by December 1941. This suggests that perhaps a greater number of Orthodox patients were being admitted or that more patients were availing themselves of the kosher option.

In addition to the listing of accounts, the board took the opportunity to remind the members of the association of how the war, which the United States had entered only a few weeks earlier, was going to cause massive upheavals: "Because of the great change in conditions throughout the world, there is no doubt that hospitals such as ours will be called upon to do their part, and certain sacrifices will have to be made by each and every one."

During World War II, the Hospital had to finish its building projects with a reduced workforce. Indeed, the Hospital faced a number of shortages as materials were diverted to the war effort. American involvement in World War I had been limited to about eighteenth months, and while several members of the staff had been called up for military service, the influenza pandemic of 1918–19 caused greater disruption to Hospital operations.

World War II was a very different matter. By the end of 1943, eighty-seven of the Hospital's physicians had been called up, including Dr. Mirsky, and this severely curtailed the work of the May Institute. One physician, Otto Salsburg Jr., was awarded the Purple Heart for wounds received in North Africa in 1943, and Aaron S. Michaelson was killed during the Battle of Savo Island (1942) when his ship, the USS *Laffey*, was sunk. In addition to the physicians, thirty-four of the nursing staff, fourteen "non-professional employees" and three members of the board of trustees were also in uniform.

Despite the disruptions and shortages of material and the call-up of staff, the Hospital continued its primary functions of serving the population of Cincinnati, training nurses and providing for the education of residents. Indeed, it was during the war that the Hospital committed itself to expanding its role as a teaching institution. Some signs of future changes can also be seen in the residency class of 1944, which not only included one woman—this was certainly not the first time that female physicians

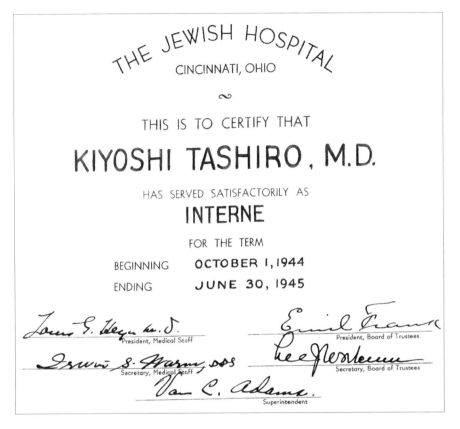

Certificate of Dr. Kiyoshi Tashiro, awarded upon completing his internship at the Jewish Hospital.

had passed through the Jewish Hospital's residency program—but also one Japanese American man.

In early 1942, almost all Japanese Americans, some 120,000 people, two-thirds of whom were U.S. citizens, were interned in federally controlled relocations centers. By 1943, some of these interns were given permission to leave the camps, provided they accepted relocation far away from their West Coast homes. A number came to Cincinnati, and one, Kiyoshi Tashiro, completed his training as an intern between October 1, 1944, and June 30, 1945. It was a portent of things to come in the postwar world, when the Jewish Hospital was among the first institutions in Cincinnati to accept African American residents.

Medical Innovators in Cincinnati: Treating Polio, Diabetes and Mental Illness in Children

To a generation that lived under the cloud of polio, Cincinnati physician Albert Sabin is a hero for developing the live virus vaccine in the 1950s. In the 1920s, long before Sabin, Cincinnati physician Albert Freiberg was also renowned for being in the forefront of treating the scourge of polio. Freiberg graduated from the University of Cincinnati's Medical School in 1890 and, as was common in that era, studied for several years in Europe before returning to Cincinnati in 1894. A professor of orthopedic surgery at the University of Cincinnati, he also served as director of orthopedic surgery at Cincinnati General, Cincinnati Children's and the Jewish Hospital. A World War I veteran, Freiberg was an active scholar who turned his attention to the treatment of polio after 1918. Freiberg's methods involved what today would be called holistic and environmental procedures, working to bolster the body's system through warm water treatments and diet. Freiberg even corresponded with Franklin D. Roosevelt, who was struck with polio in 1921; the future American president established a spa at Warm Springs, Georgia, where children could be treated, and Dr. Freiberg was a prominent consultant.

Cecil Striker was born in Kentucky and, like Freiberg, was a 1921 graduate of the University of Cincinnati Medical School. Striker, however, represented a new generation of physicians. In the late nineteenth and early twentieth centuries, graduates of American medical schools often traveled to Europe to round out their education. For Striker's generation, however, European medical education was no longer the gold standard. Striker completed his internship and residency at Cincinnati's General Hospital before he took a position as an assistant attending physician at the Jewish Hospital, where he specialized in diabetes research.

In 1934, as the storm clouds of conflict darkened around the world, Striker proposed the creation of a research institute at the Jewish Hospital. Not surprisingly, an early focus of the May Institute for Medical Research was on developing treatment for diabetes. Striker was not only a dedicated physician, but he was also one of the founders of the American Diabetes Association and served as its first president. He also had a passion for the history of medicine and in 1960 served as president of the Ohio Society of Medical History. He had a devoted interest in medical history and was the driving force behind the creation of a medical history society in Cincinnati.

The society he assembled met for the first time shortly after his death, and the society voted unanimously to name the group the Cecil Striker Society of Medical History.

As the founding director of the Psychopathic Institute, Louis Lurie was a pioneer in the treatment of mental illness in children. A specialist in neurology and psychiatry, Lurie also lectured to students on mental hygiene, a popular topic during the 1920s and '30s. In the interwar years, the welfare of children became a topic of national concern, and in 1930, Lurie was appointed by President Herbert Hoover as one of the experts to attend "A Conference on Children Health and Protection." The "Children's Charter" (1930) called on the nation to safeguard the physical and emotional well-being of children. The manifesto asserted that every child had the right to an education, the right to a stable family life and, for those who suffered physical or mental disabilities, the right to proper medical care. The charter

Plaque honoring the work of Louis Lurie on the fiftieth anniversary of the founding of the Psychopathic Institute. *Photo by author.*

ended by stating, "For Every child these rights, regardless of race, or color, or situation, wherever he may live under the protection of the flag."

These ideas likely resonated with Lurie, for they fit neatly into the mission of the Jewish Hospital. Lurie served as director of the Psychopathic Institute until 1948, and during his time at Jewish Hospital, he developed some of the earliest placebo-controlled medical trials, which resulted in new protocols for treating mental illnesses such as depression. After World War II, he served as president of the Jewish Hospital Medical Staff and was one of the founders of the American Academy of Child Psychiatry. An annual lecture at the University of Cincinnati Medical School is named in Lurie's honor.

Chapter 4

THE JEWISH HOSPITAL AFTER 1945

Adapting to a Changing World and a Crisis of Identity

O n January 9, 1956, the board of the Jewish Hospital met to discuss the future of the institution. The debate centered on a single question: "How large a hospital should the Jewish Hospital be?" While the discussion initially focused on the physical size of the institution, it quickly branched off into a wider conversation about the place of the Hospital within the Cincinnati Jewish community and its relationship to the city as a whole. As with many arguments involving Jewish life, there were multiple opinions. By the end of the debate, however, two main factions emerged.

The first faction argued that the Hospital needed to remain at its current size. The Jewish community, so the argument went, represented only about 2 percent Cincinnati's population, while 82 percent of the patients at the Hospital were not Jewish. It seemed obvious, therefore, that the Hospital was large enough to handle the needs of the Jewish community. Proponents of this faction argued that one of the reasons for maintaining the Jewish Hospital as a sectarian institution was to ensure a place for Jewish doctors to serve residencies and internships and then practice medicine. This argument harkened back to the recent past, when many medical schools restricted the number of Jewish students they admitted and many hospitals restricted the number of Jewish doctors who could practice. Although most of these restrictive practices were removed after 1945, the memory was still current in the minds of some members of the Hospital board. Some of this faction even asked whether the Jewish Hospital should be a "closed" system, where only Jewish physicians were allowed to practice.

The other faction argued that the Jewish Hospital needed to continue to expand as much as circumstances—physical and financial—would allow. This faction argued that the establishment of the Jewish Hospital in the nineteenth century was "one of the prime factors" that enabled the Jewish community to establish good relations with the rest of the city. The Hospital, they argued, should continue in this role. Since the population of Cincinnati was expanding, the Jewish Hospital needed to expand as well. This faction also pointed out that in Cincinnati there were few, if any, restrictions on Jewish medical school graduates finding internships and residencies. It further argued that as part of the Hospital's physical expansion, it should strive to achieve the highest quality of care in the region. One member of the board concluded his arguments by saying that the Jewish Hospital must always be open to new ideas and that, in order to grow, "faith in the future was necessary."

Like most discussion about the future of an institution, Jewish or gentile, the debate about the future of Cincinnati's Jewish Hospital actually tells us a great deal about the institution in 1956, as well as the issues that had shaped it in the recent past. It also tells us a great deal about the challenges and opportunities at the time of the discussion. For example, although concerns about discrimination against Jewish physicians were raised (reflecting events from the recent past), they were just as quickly countered with assertions that Jewish physicians were not being discriminated against locally (a statement about the present). While anti-Semitism in 1956 America was an issue of concern to American Jewry, it was not apparently a major concern to the board in Cincinnati. While some members of the board wanted to focus on serving the needs of the Jewish community, which was a reference to the historic mission of the Hospital, other members felt that the Hospital served an important function in integrating the Jewish community with its neighbors, a reference to the institution always being open to all regardless of race or religion. Although some feared that conflict and disaster awaited the Hospital—a very Jewish trait, some would argue—other members of the board were almost exuberant about the potential for future expansion of the Hospital.

It is also instructive to consider what issues were *not* raised. No one considered the question of whether the Hospital would continue to provide medical care to the indigent and the poor. This omission is interesting, for as we shall see, in the postwar years the number of charity patients at the Hospital declined precipitously. Furthermore, if 82 percent of the patients treated at the Hospital were not Jews, why no discussion about whether the

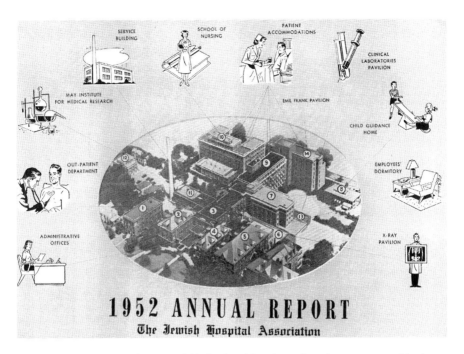

Cover pic from the annual report of 1952 advertising the various departments and institutes of the Jewish Hospital.

Hospital should continue to serve kosher food? While the overwhelming number of doctors and nurses who worked at the Hospital were Jewish, the board had voted four years earlier to allow African American physicians to serve on the medical staff. African American women also began to appear among the ranks of nursing students and, after graduation, were employed at the Hospital. It seems that just as the Hospital would treat all patients regardless of race or religion, it also would employ all, regardless of the same. Such actions not only broadened the demographic profile of the Hospital staff but also raised a question about the Jewish nature of the institution. Indeed, if the majority of patients were not Jewish, and if the staff contained a number of non-Jews, how Jewish was the Jewish Hospital? Less than a decade after this debate, the board went further and began to question whether it should elect non-Jews to serve as members of the trustees. Put this all together and it seems the future of the Jewish Hospital involved an identity crisis.

In order to understand the circumstances behind all of these debates and decisions, we need to consider the historical context of post-1945 America and the changes in the practice of medicine and hospital care.

POSTWAR CHANGES IN THE RELATIONSHIP BETWEEN GOVERNMENT AND MEDICINE

In 1945, the Jewish community of Cincinnati could look over its communal landscape and be confident that its physical and spiritual needs were met. The city had more than two dozen synagogues, covering almost all the major and minor movements within Judaism. The United Jewish Charities and Social Service Agencies ensured that philanthropic needs were addressed, while the Jewish Hospital was available to treat all manner of ailments, be they physical or mental.

The citizens of Cincinnati also had reason to regard the world with optimism. As the historian Robert Miller pointed out, World War II changed Cincinnati from a "parochial Midwestern city" into a major center of industrial production. Local firms, such as the Cincinnati Milling Machine Company (now Milacron), produced precision tools that were exported around the world. In fact, the company played an important part in the Marshall Plan, the postwar reconstruction of Europe. Like the rest of the United States, the postwar baby boom increased the population of Cincinnati. This population growth, coupled with the GI Bill, which enabled veterans to go to college and buy homes, contributed to the development of a flourishing economy. This contributed to a housing boom within the city and its environs. As the baby boomers matured, schools were built—elementary, middle, high school—to accommodate the increased number of students. While the average family size actually decreased in this era, the number of families increased dramatically. An increased number of children meant an increase in the number of medical professionals needed to care for them.

The expansion of housing and the need for services that came with the postwar boom also shifted the demographic geography of Cincinnati. Old neighborhoods such as Mount Auburn and Avondale could not meet the needs of the growing population, and as such we can see the earliest expansion to the outlying regions—the flight to the suburbs, as some scholars call it.

The war years had also transformed the relationship between the government and medical research. The effort to eradicate smallpox, malaria and especially childhood diseases such as German measles and polio were now considered high priorities by state, local and the federal government. Many private foundations, such as the Rockefeller Institute and Lily Foundation, also began directing resources to improving public

· LABORATORY · ADDITION ·
· FOR ·
· THE JEWISH HOSPITAL ASSOCIATION · CINCINNATI · O ·
· SAMUEL HANNAFORD AND SONS ·
AND
'A. LINCOLN FECHHEIMER ·
ASSOCIATED ARCHITECTS · CIN.O.

Artist rendering of the laboratory addition to the May Institute for Medical Research (early 1960s).

health. This increased funding for public health causes benefited local medical research institutions, such as the Jewish Hospital's May Institute. For example, before 1939 the May Institute for Medical Research was funded almost entirely from local sources. A bequest from the May family provided for part of its annual budget, and any additional funding had to be obtained either from local donors, private foundations or from the Hospital's operating budget.

The funding profile of the May Institute changed dramatically after 1945, as a greater number of private and government grants became available. An examination of the May Institute's budget for 1959–60 shows that while private foundations such as Pfeiffer and Loeb continued to be important sources of funding, about one-fourth of the institute's budget came from grants issued by the United States Public Health Services (USPHS). During the first quarter of 1961, this percentage rose to nearly half of the institute's income. The combination of public and private funding enabled the Hospital to devote more of its resources to expanding the May Institute's physical plant with the addition of a state-of-the-art laboratory.

Such increased funding had consequences for the direction of research. Initially, the May Institute's mandate was to provide a linkage between medical research, medical education and the treatment of patients, and early research focused on the study of diabetes, metabolic diseases and blood clotting. Although research on these topics continued, the pursuit of lucrative government grants sometimes led the institute to change the focus of its activities. For example, in the 1950s the USPHS provided grants to study the impact of radiation on the human body, not a surprising interest considering the challenges of the nuclear age and the Cold War. Although the May Institute staff had not expressed any previous interest in the study of this subject, the lure of grant money influenced them to change at least part of the direction of their research. While there was nothing dishonest in the process, and the May Institute's research certainly fit into the established medical protocols of the time, the story is instructive for illustrating the changing relationship between the federal government and medical community. There is no indication in the May Institute records that it ever conducted radiation experiments on human subjects, and it was not a part of the Cincinnati radiation experiments of the early 1960s.

World War II also transformed the relationship between the federal government and the individual. It is important to recognize that in the aftermath of the Great Depression and World War II, the role of the government in ensuring that the poor and indigent received medical care was expanded. Before 1933, poor and indigent care was primarily handled by sectarian institutions, who depended on the goodwill of their communities to provide them with the funds to aid those in need. With few exceptions, sectarian institutions provided aid to their own constituencies—for example, Catholic charities supported the poor and indigent within the Catholic community. Cincinnati's Jewish Hospital, therefore, may have been fairly unique in the United States for being a sectarian institution that provided care for all. Without detailed studies of other philanthropic organizations, it is impossible to say for certain. As we saw in previous chapters, however, the association's policy meant that it was able to draw on the financial support of people outside the Jewish community in order to serve the wider good.

By the post-1945 era, local, state and federal government were assuming a greater responsibility toward the maintenance of a basic level

May Institute for Medical Research, circa 1965.

of healthcare for the population, and this led to the establishment of Medicare and Medicaid in the 1960s. In late 1940s and '50s, however, the burden for caring for the poor and indigent was primarily borne by county governments. Medical care for the disadvantaged was handled by two interrelated methods. County governments would put levies on ballots to fund healthcare—a method still utilized today—and the tax money would be utilized by civic institutions, such as Cincinnati General Hospital, to pay for those without means. Since space and location often determined what hospital was available to treat patients, sectarian institutions like the Jewish Hospital would continue to treat charity patients. The major difference was that the Hospital could expect to be reimbursed for at least part of the cost by county government. While this system ensured greater access to medical treatment for a larger part of the population, it also meant that the historic role of institutions like the Jewish Hospital was changing, for now they were not expected to take in as many charity cases.

The implications of these changes on the basic mission of the Hospital were part of its postwar identify crisis. Should the Beckman Dispensary

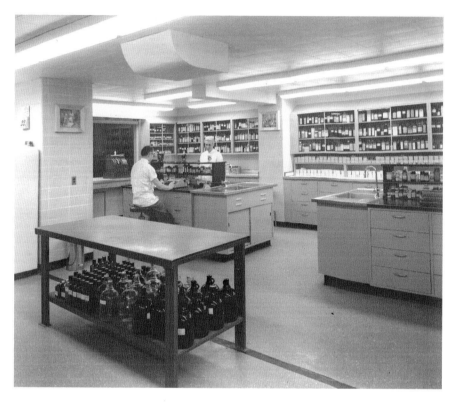

The Jewish Hospital pharmacy, circa 1970.

continue to operate if Cincinnati General Hospital was now the destination for those who could not afford to pay? If the Jewish Hospital treated charity cases and the county government failed to pass an operating levy, as happened in 1954, how would the Hospital recoup its costs? This funding system also brought the Hospital into closer contact with local political campaigns. In one case from October 1971, the Hospital board was approached by those lobbying to renew the county health levy. The local organization asked the Hospital to publicly support the campaign, for if the levy failed "the county's health care will fall to the private hospitals in the area." It also asked for a monetary contribution based on the number of beds at the Hospital ($1 for every bed, a $550 donation), and while the board refused this formula, it did ask its members to contribute to the campaign. One long-term impact of this transformation in charity care was the withering away of the activities of the Beckman Dispensary, which ceased operation in the 1970s.

On the other end of the spectrum from charity care was the rise of modern insurance in the form of Blue Cross/Blue Shield plans. Health insurance

Business office of the Jewish Hospital (mid-1960s). The volume of paperwork to run the finances of a Hospital continued to expand.

provided a sense of security for a population that feared medical costs could destroy family finances, an issue still with us today. Walter List, who served for a time as superintendent of the Jewish Hospital, saw the potential of private insurance and, according to one account, pioneered its introduction into Cincinnati. As early as 1949, the association was advocating that members of the local community sign up for Blue Cross/Blue Shield on the grounds that not only would it protect families from catastrophic costs, but it would also help ensure the fiscal health of the Hospital. In that same year, the combination of a reduction in the number of charity cases with the introduction of new insurance plans led the Hospital to revise its payment formula yet again. In this case, no mention was made of segregating charity and private patients into separate wards; instead, the focus was on payment in advance for elective procedures and setting up mechanisms for payment plans for those who could not pay the entirety of their bill immediately.

Aerial view of the Jewish Hospital in 1964, before the demolition of the old buildings.

Despite charity cases being shifted to Cincinnati General Hospital, the city found itself facing a prolonged crisis brought on by the lack of space. By the 1950s, all hospitals had provisions for emergency services; the challenge, it turned out, was in meeting non-emergency needs. For private patients who paid cash or had insurance, there was an expectation that they were entitled to hospital services—if not immediately upon request then within a short time. By the mid-1950s, however, a shortage of beds meant that hospitals were forced to categorize needs according to a three-tier system: "Medical Urgent," "Surgical Urgent" and "Surgical Elective." Throughout the late 1950s and '60s, the superintendent of the Jewish Hospital kept a monthly total of the wait time for those who required hospitalization. In April 1965, the superintendent's report listed the wait time as follows:

- Medical Urgent   25 Days
- Surgical Urgent   19 Days
- Surgical Elective   42 Days

The lobby of the old Jewish Hospital building shortly before demolition.

These numbers would vary over the next four years from a low wait time for Medical Urgent of 17 days in February 1969 to a staggering 117-day wait for Surgical Elective in the same month. At one point in 1966, as complaints about the wait time grew, the chairman of the Hospital board remarked that his doctor recommended he have back surgery, and yet even he was expected to wait 60 days before he could be treated. Such comments were not likely to mollify angry customers. According to reports, the bed shortage was a citywide problem; therefore, the only way to solve it was to either build new hospitals or expand existing facilities.

Before 1945, Jewish Hospital construction projects were funded through donations, the selling of bonds or direct borrowing from banks. Occasionally, the sale of old properties could also add to building funds. This did not always work out as planned. For example, in 1890, the association planned on using the proceeds from the sale of the original Hospital building on Third and Baum to pay down the debt on the new building. Unfortunately,

Dr. Othilda Krug was director of the Child Guidance Home, later the Child Psychiatric Center, from 1948 to 1983. She was perhaps the first woman to head a major institute of the Jewish Hospital.

the board found itself unable to sell the original property for reasons that remain unclear. In the early twentieth century, it gave up trying to sell the building and ceded it to a Catholic orphanage. An ecumenical gesture, but not one that benefited the balance sheet of the association.

While charity cases were increasingly encouraged to go to Cincinnati General, state and local governments recognized that some aspects of public health were still being carried out by the private sector. In the 1960s, the Child Guidance Home was one of the few branches of the association that continued to serve a high percentage of charity cases. As we saw in the previous chapter, child welfare, including mental health, had become an important priority in the United States. When the Jewish Hospital proposed expanding the Child Guidance Home, it found that it could draw on a substantial amount of government money to assist in the project. The total budget for building the new facility was $847,990. While $351,792 had been raised locally, the Hospital obtained $405,908 as a grant from the State of Ohio. Now, while this left a balance of $117,289, a substantial sum to be sure, it should not obscure the fact that approximately half the cost came from government funding. It was during this project, in 1968, that the Child Guidance Home was renamed Children's Psychiatric Center.

In 1968, the Jewish Hospital also began implementing its plans for a massive change to the Burnet Avenue facility. Unlike previous work, this would not be expansion or modifications, but rather a complete tear-down of the 1890 building in order to replace it with a modern structure. Concerned about having to raise a great deal of money led the board on October 2, 1967, to raise the question of whether it should recruit non-Jewish members. Some argued that this would expand the potential donor pool beyond the Jewish community and make possible greater utilization of public funds, as was

CHILD GUIDANCE HOME — 1958

OTHILDA KRUG, M.D., Director

Article by Dr. Othilda Krug announcing the planned expansion of the Child Guidance Home in the 1958 issue of the *Cincinnati Medical Journal*. It took more than a decade for the expansion to be finished.

Promotional brochure for the renovated and expanded Jewish Hospital complex.

Reception area of the Jewish Hospital, circa 1918. Notice the checkerboard tile on the floor.

Reception area of the Jewish Hospital in 1967. The original tiles remained until demolition.

Utensils and dishes from the Hospital's kosher kitchen. According to dietary law, dishes can only be used for meat or dairy, not both.

being done with the newly renamed Children's Psychiatric Center. In the end, the board chose not to change its ethnic composition, although it did appeal to the general Cincinnati community for funds.

The Burnet Avenue building had stood for about eighty years, and its endurance can be seen in a comparison of photographs of the lobby: the first image shows the reception area in about 1918 and the second the same location right before the demolition. If one looks at the floor, we can see that the tile was original. Right before the demolition, the association removed the Jewish Hospital sign from the entryway; the plan was to place it over the new entrance when building was complete. The construction project also focused on something that no one in 1890 probably every thought of dealing with: a shortage of parking spaces. Fully one quarter of the board's discussions about plans dealt with this issue. The new building contained all the necessary components for maintaining Jewish ritual life, in particular

Demolition of the original Burnet Avenue Hospital building in 1968.

a kosher kitchen and a Brit Milah room. Ironically, the more the Hospital struggled with the question of how Jewish it was, the more it devoted itself to serving the needs of its Jewish patients, even if they represented less than 20 percent of the total.

RACE RELATIONS

In 1894, the board of the Jewish Hospital received a message from a Mrs. Laura Strauss, "asking if a Colored pay patient can be admitted to the hospital." After due consideration, it was resolved that "as soon as the painting and cleaning of the Hospital was completed, which would take several weeks, the Board would be ready to receive Mrs. Wilson [the patient in question]."

Entry in the minutes of the board of trustees of the Jewish Hospital from 1952 relating to the appointment of African American physicians.

No specific malady or request for treatment was identified in the minutes, and no explanation as to what part of the Hospital was being painted and cleaned or why it would take several weeks to finish was made. Yet this brief entry is one of the few references to race relations in the Hospital records prior to the 1950s. It is not that African Americans are completely absent from the story of the Hospital—remember that in the 1920s Louis Levy's administrative reforms called for the hiring of two "colored" maids. One oral history brought to the author's attention claimed that African American patients were treated at the Hospital throughout the 1920s. To date, however, no documentary evidence can be found to substantiate the claim. It is possible that Levy's segregated ward plan of 1920 was based on more than ability to pay, but again the records are silent about racial issues.

This silence was abruptly shattered on March 23, 1952, when the board issued a simple statement that read in part: "[T]hat colored physicians be appointed to the staff on the same basis as white physicians." We have already seen an example of a non-Jewish physician serving as an intern when Kiyoshi Tashiro completed his training in 1945. Yet this was a distinctly new frontier for the Hospital, and it occurred at a time when few other institutions were willing to take African American interns or residents.

Even the presence of a Japanese American as an intern was not necessarily a sign of racial progress. During the early civil rights era, many hospitals would take Asian Americans as means of filling their complement of students and as a means of avoiding the need to employ an African American physician. Simply put, while in the late nineteenth century Cincinnati was a center of aggressive union activity and in the early twentieth century was in the forefront of progressive ideas, by the 1950s the city did not have a very distinguished record of civil rights.

Fortunately, part of the backstory to the admission of African Americans to the medical staff can be gleaned from Hospital records. In early May 1952, Mrs. Virginia Coffey, of the "Mayor's Friendly Relations Committee," wrote to David Ross, the Hospital superintendent. In the letter, she referenced both a recent article in the *Call and Post* (a mayoral newsletter) and a recent conference held at the Jewish Hospital between the board and the Urban League. In the 1950s, the Urban League, a social service agency dedicated to promoting opportunities for African Americans, was actively promoting the placement of African American physicians into private hospitals.

Mamie McGrady   Thomas Muething   Jane Oldham

Martha Schauer   Barbara Simpson   Leslie Smith

Part of the nursing school's graduating class of 1972, showing the results of racial and gender integration. By the 1970s, the nursing school had graduated several dozen African American women.

The article, dated March 25 (two days after the board's announcement) celebrated an award from the Cincinnati Urban League to the Jewish Hospital for its work in promoting race relations. The Urban League was fulsome in its praise: "We knew it was non-sectarian, that Negroes worked there and were admitted as patients. But we had no idea how completely integrated they were until we talked with David Ross, the young superintendent."

According to the article, the Hospital had six African American physicians on staff, along with four student nurses, four practical nurses and eleven nurses' aides. In addition to the medical staff, there were African American laboratory technicians, kitchen workers, dietitians, household workers and a cook in the Child Guidance Home. Now that the Hospital had agreed to accept applicants from accredited medical colleges, it would likely have its first African American intern. The presence of African American employees

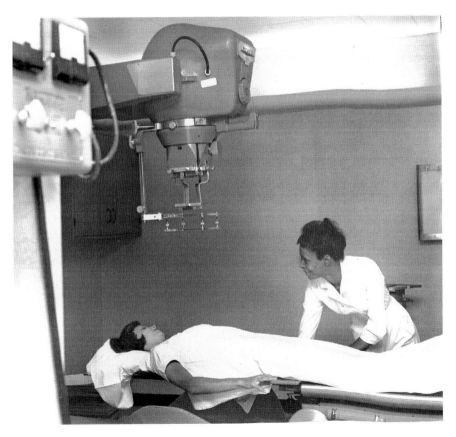

African American X-ray technician at the Jewish Hospital, circa 1970.

on the support staff is not surprising—kitchen and cleaning staff were, after all, common jobs for minorities. How long the African American physicians had been on staff is not known. Since the Hospital nursing program, which ran for three years, often hired its own graduates, and since the African American nurses were identified as students, it is likely that they had been accepting them since the late 1940s.

After lauding the work conditions and the lack of segregation in the patient wards, the article concluded:

> *This is an amazing record for any hospital, but especially for a private one in Cincinnati. Other private hospitals in our city may well take lessons on how it can be done, for Jewish Hospital has forged way ahead of most of them…when Dr. Ross was asked about the secret of their success, he replied: "It's simple. We take people here solely on the basis of their qualification. We only take the best."*

What is clear from the article is that the association had done a great deal to improve race relations within the Hospital before the formal announcement in March 1953. Apparently, it did a poor job of publicizing these efforts outside the Hospital setting, understandable perhaps given how tense race relations could be in the city.

AN ERA ENDS

The acute bed shortage that so obsessed Jewish Hospital administrators began to ease by the mid-1970s. In part this was due to the expanded facility on Burnet Avenue and in part to the opening of new hospitals in the northeast and northwest sections of the city. The Jewish Hospital of the 1970s was a much different entity than the one dedicated eighty years earlier. Its physical plant was dominated by a new structure of modern design. The Hospital's staff were in the forefront of medical technology, for example being among the first to carry out open-heart surgical procedures in Cincinnati. A century earlier, the Hospital routinely provided tobacco for patients, at a cost. In the 1970s, the physicians led a campaign to stop tobacco sales at the Hospital, for they did not "feel it proper to give its good will to cigarette smoking." Even the sale of alcohol was discontinued.

Emergency treatment room of the Jewish Hospital in the early 1970s.

In retrospect, we know that the days of the Jewish Hospital at its historic location were numbered. In 1890, the area that came to be known as Pill Hill was sparsely settled and yet easily accessible to both working-class and bourgeois neighborhoods of Mount Auburn, Avondale and Clifton. It was physically close to the University of Cincinnati, whose Medical School played such a dominant role in the life of the Hospital.

By the 1960s and '70s, Pill Hill was a congested area, home to half a dozen hospitals, university buildings and the attendant traffic problems that still plague the area. Of greater concern to Hospital administrators was the deterioration of the Mount Auburn and Avondale neighborhoods. By the 1960s, most of the Jewish community had moved from these environs, mostly north along the I-71 corridor or northeast to the neighborhoods of Amberly Village and Blue Ash. Furthermore, race riots had decimated parts of the neighborhoods around Pill Hill, and some regarded making a trip to the Hospital as a worrying proposition.

New Jewish Hospital building on Burnet Avenue in the early 1970s.

The lobby of the new Jewish Hospital Building in the early 1970s.

The announcement that the Jewish Hospital was building a new facility in the Kenwood area, some ten and a half miles to the northeast, surprised some. The facility was initially justified, at least in part, as a way of serving the changing geographic pattern of the community. It was also argued that it would help reduce the strain on the existing institution, should a shortage of beds reoccur.

In May 1995, the Jewish Hospital was sold to the new Cincinnati Health Alliance. The goal of the alliance was to pool the resources of the various hospitals, thereby improving access to healthcare for city residents. Benjamin Gettler, the last chair of the board of the Jewish Hospital, oversaw the sale and then oversaw the creation the Jewish Foundation of Cincinnati. By this point, only half the beds in the Burnet Avenue building were being used. To the surprise of few, the Health Alliance announced that the Burnet Avenue buildings would cease hospital activities as of November 1997. While the building remained an administrative center for several more years, its future seemed uncertain.

Medical Portraits: Cincinnati Physicians in a Changing World

The intern and resident class of 1947–48 was the first class to complete school and training after the end of World War II. The students were entering a medical profession that was undergoing a number of changes, not just in treatment and new technology but in how physicians interacted with both the public and the administrations of the hospitals in which they served. Of the twenty-six residents and interns to serve at the Jewish Hospital between 1947 and 1948, the only woman was Rachel Braunstein. Most have distinctive Jewish names, and a majority matriculated at the University of Cincinnati Medical School. Rachel Braunstein completed her studies as an intern in 1948 and a year later qualified as a radiologist at the Hospital. While she was not the first female physician at the Jewish Hospital, she was, however, one of a growing number of women to enter the field of medicine. She represents how the times were beginning to change. Over the next few years, more women and members of minority groups would pass through the Hospital.

Before moving to Cincinnati, Albert Sabin earned his MD from New York University and worked for the Rockefeller Institute for Medical Research. In

Composite photograph of the interns and residents of the Jewish Hospital, 1947–48.

1939, he was appointed an associate professor of pediatrics at the University of Cincinnati College of Medicine, and except for service in World War II, he remained at the University of Cincinnati until 1969.

When Sabin began his research on poliomyelitis, few practical treatments existed. As we saw in a previous chapter, Albert Freiberg experimented with methods of treatment for patients with polio; however, no practical

THE JEWISH HOSPITAL
CINCINNATI, OHIO

∞

THIS IS TO CERTIFY THAT

Rachel W. Braunstein, M.D.

HAS SERVED SATISFACTORILY AS

Resident in Radiology

FOR THE TERM

BEGINNING   JULY 1, 1948

ENDING   JUNE 30, 1949

_____   _____
President, Medical Staff   President, Board of Trustees

Nathan J. Kursban, M.D.   _____
Secretary, Medical Staff   Secretary, Board of Trustees

_____
Superintendent

Rachel Braunstein's certification of completion in radiology from the Jewish Hospital. A year earlier, she had finished her internship.

Dr. Albert Sabin in his laboratory at the University of Cincinnati Medical School.

method of immunization existed. Sabin's research was part of larger studies he conducted on other viruses that caused diseases of the nervous system. In 1954, Jonas Salk's "dead virus" vaccine was put into use throughout the United States and had a dramatic effect on the number of children affected. Sabin believed that only a "live virus"—in other words, a weakened strain of poliomyelitis—would provide long-term immunity. Since Salk's virus was adopted as the standard protocol in the United States, Sabin's virus was tested and then distributed overseas starting in 1960s. Although Sabin, like Salk, patented the vaccine, both made the patents available to all. Unlike Salk, who was more famous in the popular imagination but whose post-polio vaccine career seemed to sputter, Sabin continued working on treatments for a variety of viruses.

EPILOGUE

Hiram B. Weis's (1890–1982) career as a physician in the Cincinnati Jewish community followed a recognizable trajectory. Like many of his contemporaries, he studied medicine at the University of Cincinnati, graduating in 1915, before serving his residency at the newly completed Cincinnati General Hospital. After residency, he worked with the Beckman Dispensary and played an important part in expanding its relationship with the Jewish Hospital. Weis was then elected an attending physician in internal medicine at the Jewish Hospital, eventually serving as president of the Hospital's Medical Staff, as well as director of internal medicine. Weis also taught internal medicine at the University of Cincinnati, following a well-worn path between the two institutions. Weis's daughter, Regine, married William Ransohoff, a physician and grandson of Joseph Ransohoff, who played such an important role in the development of the medical staff of the Jewish Hospital.

Weis published widely in his specialty and was also fascinated by the history of medicine in Cincinnati, details of which he recounted in a 1971 article for the *Cincinnati Journal of Medicine*. Weis was also fascinated by medical artifacts, and his collection of historic stethoscopes was displayed in a wall case in the Jewish Hospital library for a number of years. When the Burnet Avenue building was closed in 1997, the fate of much of the Jewish Hospital's records, including the stethoscope collection, became unknown.

In 2013, I was asked to accompany Doris Haag, then chief archivist for the Winkler Center for the History of Allied Health Professions, to gather

Dr. Hiram Weis with his stethoscope collection. Unfortunately, most of the collection was lost when the Burnet Avenue building was closed.

what remnants of the Jewish Hospital records and artifacts still remained in the Burnet Avenue building. At that time, the future of the building was in doubt, as it had been acquired by UC Medical, and discussions had only just begun as to what to do with the space. When we entered the old library and found the wall case, all that remained of the stethoscope collection were a few pieces of rotting rubber. No one at the Jewish Hospital or the Jewish Foundation knew what had happened to Weis's collection. To some the disappearance of this collection is a metaphor for what they fear is the loss of the Jewish history of the Cincinnati Jewish Hospital.

Some say that the past is prologue. As such, we end where we began, with the Jewish Hospital now being run by the Catholic Mercy Health organization and the question of whether its heritage and identity are in danger of being lost. Certainly a great deal was lost in the move from Pill Hill to the Kenwood location, the Weis collection being just one example. It is unfair, however, to blame the wastage of the Hospital's heritage on

The Jewish Hospital Building on Burnet Avenue in 2015. The building is now part of UC Medical. *Photo by author.*

Stone tablets from the old Jewish Hospital building now sit in the lower basement on Burnet Avenue. Their continued safety is a challenge to preservationists. *Photo by author.*

more recent history alone. When the old building on Burnet Avenue was demolished in the late 1960s, the stone tablets that commemorate the early donors were removed and eventually ended up in a room in the lower basement, where they remain. Fortunately, while the building may have

Jewish Hospital Building on Galbraith Road in the Kenwood neighborhood of Cincinnati. As with most hospitals, construction is a near constant feature. *Photo by author.*

passed through various owners over the previous thirty years, key members of the maintenance staff remained. These men have done what they could to protect the precious artifacts. While a number of people would like to see them preserved, and even perhaps exhibited to the public, as of the writing of this volume no concrete plans have been proposed.

The current home of the Jewish Hospital of Cincinnati sits just over eleven miles from its original location near the riverfront of Third and Baum. Yet the current building and the historic facility are worlds apart, separated not just by distance and time. As you walk the hallways near the entranceway of the Kenwood building, the walls are covered with commemorative plaques celebrating lay leaders who sponsored buildings and physicians who dedicated their professional lives to the institution. That part of the heritage of the Hospital will remain as long as people can stop and read them. Although it is run by a Catholic organization, the Jewish Hospital not only retains its name but also has a permanent rabbinic chaplaincy, as well as the availability of kosher food. Such things are taken for granted now but were of more recent extraction. Perhaps it is fair to say that the character of the Hospital is more Jewish now that it has ever been.

BIBLIOGRAPHY

Bonner, Thomas Neville. *Iconoclast: Abraham Flexner and a Life in Learning.* Baltimore, MD: Johns Hopkins University Press, 2002.

Brown, Theodore M. "Jewish Physicians in the United States." *Jews and Medicine: Religion, Culture, Science.* Edited by Natalie Berger. New York: Jewish Publication Society, 1995.

Fine, John, and Frederic Krome. *The Jews of Cincinnati.* Charleston, SC: Arcadia Publishing, 2007.

Goss, Charles Frederic. *Cincinnati, the Queen City, 1788–1912.* Cincinnati, OH: S.J. Clarke Publishing, 1912.

Greve, Charles Theodore. *Centennial History of Cincinnati and Representative Citizens.* 2 vols. Cincinnati, OH: Biographical Publishing, 1904.

Haller, John S., Jr. *A Profile in Alternate Medicine: The Eclectic Medical College of Cincinnati, 1845–1942.* Kent, OH: Kent State University Press, 1999.

Kraut, Alan, and Deborah A. Kraut. *Covenant of Care: Newark Beth Israel and the Jewish Hospital in America.* New Brunswick, NJ: Rutgers University Press, 2007.

Miller, Robert E. *World War II Cincinnati: From the Front Lines to the Home Front.* Charleston, SC: The History Press, 2014.

Miller, Zane. *Boss Cox's Cincinnati: Urban Politics in the Progressive Era.* New York: Oxford University Press, 1970.

Porter, Roy. "Hospitals and Surgery." *The Cambridge History of Medicine.* Edited by Roy Porter. New York: Cambridge University Press, 2006.

———. "Mental Illness." *The Cambridge History of Medicine.* Edited by Roy Porter. New York: Cambridge University Press, 2006.

Ramsden, Edmund. "Science and Medicine in the United States of America." *The Oxford Handbook of the History of Medicine.* New York: Oxford University Press, 2011.

Sarna, Jonathan. *American Judaism: A History.* New Haven, CT: Yale University Press, 2004.

———. "'A Sort of Paradise for the Hebrews': The Lofty Vision of Cincinnati Jews." *Ethnic Diversity and Civic Identity: Patterns of Conflict and Cohesion in Cincinnati Since 1820.* Edited by Henry D. Shapiro and Jonathan D. Sarna. Champaign: University of Illinois Press, 1992.

Sarna, Jonathan, and Nancy Klein. *The Jews of Cincinnati.* Cincinnati, OH: Center for the American Jewish Experience, 1989.

Selya, Roger, and Alysha Beyer. "Where Do We Go Now? Issues in Establishing a Dominant Jewish Neighborhood in Cincinnati, Ohio." *Land and Community: Geography in Jewish Studies.* Potomac: University Press of Maryland, 1997.

Shorter, Edward. "Primary Care." *The Cambridge History of Medicine.* Edited by Roy Porter. New York: Cambridge University Press, 2006.

Stradling, David. *Smokestacks and Progressives: Environmentalists, Engineers and Air Quality in America, 1881–1951.* Baltimore, MD: Johns Hopkins University Press, 1999.

Striker, Cecil. *Medical Portraits.* Cincinnati, OH: Academy of Medicine Cincinnati, 1963.

Weibe, Robert. *The Search for Order, 1877–1920.* New York: Hill & Wang, 1967.

Winkler, Allan. "The Queen City and World War II." *Queen City Heritage* (Spring 1991).

INDEX

ABOUT THE AUTHOR

Frederic Krome was born in Germany to a military family, was raised in various locations on the East Coast and has lived in Cincinnati since 1986. Krome earned his PhD in history from the University of Cincinnati in 1992. He taught at Northern Kentucky University from 1992 to 1998, was managing editor of the *American Jewish Archives Journal* for eight years and since 2007

Photo by Mikki Schaffer.

has taught history at the University of Cincinnati Clermont College. His publications include *The Jews of Cincinnati* (with John Fine) and *Fighting the Future War: An Anthology of Science Fiction War Stories, 1914–45*. He currently resides in the Cincinnati neighborhood of College Hill with his wife, Claire; two Pembroke corgis; and two crazy cats.

Visit us at
www.historypress.net
....
This title is also available as an e-book